Hertfordshire

J want to
Oxbridge?
ne about
anana...

idge applications

First published in Great Britain in 2005 by

Oxbridge Applications
13-14 New Bond Street
London W1S 3SX

ISBN 0-9550797-1-3

Contents

Preface

By James Uffindell

What is it about Oxford and Cambridge? What is it about these two Universities that inspires such conflicting passions among students, parents and teachers, in the press, in the government and the country as a whole? Why do the alumni from these two Universities dominate Parliament, Medicine and the world of business?

The answer is simple: like it or not, in days gone by Oxbridge was unquestionably the best. But does former grandeur translate into modern-day dominance? And if it does, what does that mean for the people who don't make it and the people who do? Whilst these two institutions were undoubtedly the world leaders in Higher Education a hundred years ago, there's an argument that they've now lost the plot; redundant, anachronistic and living on past glories. Attempts to modernise, such as the failed proposed reforms of Oxford's governing body by the Vice Chancellor, Dr John Hood, are fiercely resisted. Like the House of Lords, people claim that Oxbridge exists for what it was, not what it is.

However the fact remains that Oxford and Cambridge are still two of the world's leading educational institutions. The Times Good University Guide 2007 has Oxford at number one and Cambridge at number two. A 2006 study of the World's Top 500 universities[1] puts Cambridge as the second best institution, whilst Oxford is tenth (the next highest ranked British institution, Imperial, only makes it in at number 23).

[1] By Shanghai Jiao Tong University, 2006

Oxbridge also provides a unique educational experience through the intensity of its tutorial/supervision system. Small group teaching, with students being taught to communicate their ideas with an academic, is an obvious catalyst to increased confidence. If students are constantly required to articulate, defend, think through and adapt their ideas under the most rigorous intellectual cross-examination by some of the brightest minds in the world, and they still survive, it makes negotiation in the real world a walk in the park. Other attributes of the Universities only add to their very real credentials: their abilities to attract excellent teaching staff, high-graduate starting salaries, generous financial support packages for students and the sheer beauty of the cities make them highly attractive places to study.

Modern day accusations of snobbery (Oxford was rumoured to have invented the word 'snob' when tutors used to write 's.nob' (sine nobilitate - meaning 'without noble birth') on the exam papers of applicants) lack credibility. Whilst Oxbridge's statistics of being roughly 50:50 state:independent students may look scandalous when compared with a national ratio of 90:10 for the population of 17 year-olds as a whole, the Universities take on approximately the same proportions as they receive applications. The fault, from this diagnosis, lies not with the Universities in their acceptance of bright students from the state-sector who do apply, but with getting the students to apply in the first place. Who applies to Oxford and Cambridge is not ultimately determined by the Universities themselves (though they obviously have a strong role to play), but more by teachers and parents and individual students. Despite the challenges that Oxford and Cambridge face, such as competing institutions, government attempts at social-engineering and funding issues, they remain respected and revered academic institutions that have moved with the times, and are constantly striving to maintain their momentum.

I never thought I could get into Oxbridge. Both my parents left school at 16. The two uncles I did have who went to Oxford possessed an almost 'golden halo' by sheer virtue of the fact that they had studied there. Growing up, Oxbridge was always placed on an academic pedestal, one I never thought I would be able to mount. It was for other people rather than me. I was the boy who sat at the back of the class and got away with doing as little as possible. Then three things happened to me. Firstly, I got my GCSE results and I realised that all my friends had been working, whilst I had been doing what most 16 year olds do - playing on my Super Nintendo, hanging out at the shopping centre on a Saturday and watching TV. I realised that I deserved better than I had got and never again wanted to let myself down. Secondly, I started studying subjects that really interested me for my A-levels. Thirdly, an inspirational young teacher joined the school and made me realise just what I was capable of doing if I put my mind to it. This combination of a competitive streak, being passionate about my subjects and having the support I really needed in mentoring me through the application process proved a winning combination. I overcame what we see as the five major hurdles to getting an offer:

1. I applied to a less than averagely competitive college

2. I did lots of reading around my subject

3. I put time into my personal statement

4. I produced strong written work

5. I made sure that I would feel comfortable talking to people I didn't know about my subject

Looking back, it was all quite simple. It wasn't that I was cleverer than other applicants (other applicants from my school, who were brighter than me, failed to get offers for my course), it was just that I put a lot of effort into the areas of the application that really mattered. I also applied with a mindset that I would do the whole thing properly. Then, if I didn't get in I knew I would have no regrets and I would still be going to a good university. Getting the offer letter was a fantastic experience, though not nearly as good as my three years at Oxford.

Seven years after leaving Oxford our organisation, Oxbridge Applications, has helped over 30,000 applicants with their applications. Through the sheer weight of numbers, and having a superb team working full time on the applications process we've learnt a lot about what makes one applicant succeed and another fail. Working with teachers, students, parents and ex-admissions tutors gives us a unique view of the process and puts us in a unrivalled position of expertise as to what it really takes to get an offer. Our success rates show the qualities we have developed. Not everyone approves of what we do: the Universities think that applicants shouldn't need to have help with their applications. In a perfect world they wouldn't. We believe that people have the right to make the most of themselves and if they're applying for something they deem to be important then why shouldn't they prepare to the best of their abilities? By 'prepare' I don't mean that applicants should become something they're not; I simply mean they should get used to articulating and discussing their ideas in an unfamiliar environment. Applicants should channel their academic focus efficiently so that they can enjoy their subject to the fullest.

The Oxbridge interview is often the first interview a 17 year-old has had and it can be daunting. To anyone who says that practice doesn't improve interview performance, I would ask them to name one other test where performance doesn't improve with experience. I'm proud of the work we do helping students fulfil their potential. I'm also proud of all the bright students who, with our support, are able to show tutors just how good they really are, rather than failing to exhibit their full potential. Our job is to lift the tops of treasure chests so that tutors can see how good applicants really our - we do this exceptionally well.

The students we help come from all sectors of society - we will not allow money to be a barrier to students benefiting from our services. We do extensive work with schools through the government's Aimhigher programme and our Access Scheme helps approximately 100 students a year free of charge - full details are available on our website.

We first published 'So you want to go to Oxbridge? Tell me about a banana...' in 2005, this is the second updated edition. I hope you find the book useful for your application. We outline why you might want to be considering Oxbridge in the first place and what you should be doing to maximise your chances. With the help of stories from and references to Alan Partridge, Tony Blair and Ali G, we'll try to give you the insights you need to do as well as you possibly can. Good luck with the application and if you have any queries please contact me.

James Uffindell
Company Founder
james.uffindell@oxbridgeapplications.com
July 2007

Foreword

by Barry Webb

Having spent over ten years involved with university admissions processes, I can sympathise with the anxieties and hopes of prospective candidates. The competition for a place at Oxford or Cambridge has never been fiercer. Many school-leavers feel that the odds are stacked against them and that only those who have some privileged access can ever be successful. Extra tests and the prospect of an interview can make potentially successful candidates give up before they begin. They feel that there is some 'secret formula' or 'hidden key' that is denied to them. This is entirely untrue: anybody with the right qualifications has an equal chance of success and what may seem from the outside to be a system slanted in favour of those who can somehow "buy" success is in fact a system designed to select the best candidates regardless of their background. If you want to apply and have the appropriate grades you have as good a chance as anyone else.

The interview system is in fact a leveller. You are treated as an individual and not a statistic, and it is a level playing-field for all candidates once you are in the room. The universities do not have any hidden agenda or favoured type of candidate. All they want are the best people who offer themselves on the day. And by "best" they don't mean just the person with the most crammed knowledge - they are looking for all-round intellectual ability linked with academic curiosity and commitment. Nobody can obtain these things over the counter; they are intrinsic to any individual who is prepared to stretch themselves to the limit and aim for the highest. Background is irrelevant.

There are several reasons for the present competitive situation, and they pose problems for both candidates and the universities. The nub of the problem is that many more school-leavers have attained the 3 A grades which are the most common entrance requirements for Oxbridge. The colleges, however, have no more places to offer. Since, at present, there no gradations within the "A" bracket to distinguish between a top or lower "A", the universities must inevitably look elsewhere to sift through an already highly impressive pool in order to narrow their choice in as fair and efficient a way as possible. The two obvious options open to them are (1) to set an extra test of their own during the entrance process and (2) to make ever more use of the interview as a selection tool.

A difficult situation inevitably arises. The universities wish to gauge by use of test and interview those things which the A-Level and U.C.A.S. form cannot properly reveal (such as potential and motivation): things which by definition cannot be prepared for, thus revealing innate qualities that haven't been taught and which cannot be bought by candidates with greater access to facilities or specialist teaching. The tests will tend to concentrate on how you apply your mind rather than your ability to recall facts, and how you can think under pressure. All candidates (and parents), however, will immediately ask themselves "how can I "prepare" for these extra hurdles?"

It is clear that at one level the answer is, "You can't, nor should you be able to". That is, you cannot change your personality nor suddenly improve your academic and intellectual potential overnight. What you can do is to consult those whose experience can help you to show yourself - as you are now - to your best possible advantage. This is what Oxbridge Applications is aiming to do. Nobody is offering a "magic key" or "secret formula", because none exists. What is on offer is a wide range of expertise to help you both to play to your strengths and to avoid the pitfalls that so many able people fall into, thus preventing the interviewer from getting a true impression of their abilities.

It is important to realise that the interview is intended to discover what is unique about yourself; not how you fit into some pre-conceived mould. Your U.C.A.S. form will have shown how much you know about the basics of the subject you have chosen to study so the interview is unlikely to concentrate entirely on this. More important is showing how you react to academic and intellectual challenges. The interviewer will want to judge how much you are likely to develop over three or four years. You need to be able to show that you are a committed and engaged candidate; if you aren't you should not be entering the competition!

This is not a conveyor belt - the admissions process is about individuality not conformity - and there is no brain-washing or attempting to beat the system; as explained that would be as unethical as it is impossible. What is possible is to raise your game by sensible discussion and advice.

It has been a pleasure to see so many candidates from a variety of backgrounds improve their chances by this common-sense approach. The success rate suggests that it has been a valuable experience for many. But remember: others can offer advice; only you can turn advice into success.

Barry Webb
Member of Oxbridge Applications Advisory Board
barry.webb@oxbridgeapplications.com
July 2007

What is so great about Oxbridge?

The Universities of Oxford and Cambridge were both founded in the 13th century: University College was the first Oxford College, founded in 1249 by William of Durham, and Peterhouse was the first Cambridge College, founded in 1284 by Hugo De Balsham, Bishop of Ely. The emergence of Oxbridge, however, is more difficult to pin down. The key thing when applying is to remember that Oxbridge exists only as a brand name. Oxbridge constitutes a brand identity that has been built over hundreds of years, that resonates in the characters of Chaucer's sneaky clerks, and echoes down Waugh's shady cloisters. It is perpetuated by the alumni, who tend to enjoy the air of mystery and excellence that surrounds their education, by the faculties which benefit from millions of pounds in funding as well as attracting the finest students and researchers, and by local businesses, who profit from an unrivalled concentration of foreign tourists, all keen to get a glimpse into the exotic Oxbridge mystery. It is a phenomenon best illustrated by events such as the Oxford and Cambridge boat race, where hundreds of thousands of people with no interest whatsoever in this relatively obscure sport settle down in their armchairs to cheer on the heroics of two groups of young students, and perhaps to share for an afternoon in the glamour of the Oxbridge experience.

Perhaps the most important unifying feature of successful applicants is a genuine desire to succeed. You have to want it. With this in mind, it's worth taking a brief look at some of the features that make Oxford and Cambridge two of the best universities in the world and why they are worth fighting for.

The Tutorial/Supervision System

As a result of excellent funding and an exceptionally high ratio of staff to students, Oxbridge is able to run the tutorial/supervision in addition to the normal programme of lectures and seminars. Tutorials (as they are called at Oxford) or supervisions (as they are called at Cambridge) are generally one or two hour sessions that take place anywhere from the academic's rooms to the local Starbucks (though you are unlikely to be meeting your Professor of Marxist Studies and Post-Colonial Multiculturalism there!) The academic in question will be an expert in your chosen field of study, selected for you by your Director of Studies (DOS, Cambridge) or tutor (Oxford) from your college. The number of students present at these weekly meetings can be as large as four or five, but generally the groups consist of only one or two. Tutorials are shared with students from the same year group and (sometimes) college. Their purpose is to discuss that week's reading, the ideas it raised, and the successes and failures of each student's weekly essay. Oxford and Cambridge, though they have shorter terms than almost any other university, work their students very hard, and about three essays a fortnight (and the equivalent in problems to solve for the scientists) is standard. As one academic famously put it, 'If I am to cure you of your ignorance, your weekly essay must be like a urine sample: copious and all yours.' Though quality of thought is always more important than quantity, you may be expected to produce a certain volume of writing or solutions to problems.

The tutorial/supervision system has several major advantages, and contributes to the high regard in which Oxbridge graduates are held by employers: firstly, and most significantly, it teaches students to formulate verbal arguments. To get the most from the discursive format of the tutorial, a student has to learn to voice their opinions coherently, to ask cogent questions, and to defend their points of view from marauding critics. This is particularly important in small groups, where heated debates between individuals complement the guidance and authority of the academic conducting the discussion. Over three or four years of study, this system can turn even the most shy and retiring of intellectuals into a formidable and persuasive speaker, and an attentive listener. This is true of bespectacled scientists and floppy-haired aesthetes alike. Also, for those who never quite get around to doing the required reading, the chance to hone your skills in holding forth on a subject about which you know next to nothing can also prove very useful - it's interesting that so many MPs attended Oxbridge! The discursive element of the tutorial system in turn influences the interview process; the kinds of people who will benefit most from and contribute most to tutorials will be those who are willing to expound their own views, and to listen constructively to the views of others.

The second great advantage of the tutorial system is the sheer level of personal attention afforded to each student. Very few universities in the world can compete with Oxbridge on these terms. Personal, intimate communication with a world expert in your field of study inspires hard work and gives you the deepest possible insight into your subject. Because you have the chance to discuss your written work, problems of style and content are more easily corrected, and your supervisor and tutor can guide you away from bad habits over a period of weeks and months. Such is the dominance of the tutorial system at Oxbridge that, whilst it is designed to run alongside lectures, many students (particularly in the humanities) eschew the lecture halls entirely and concentrate all their energies on the reading and issues that arise from their tutorials. Of course we do not condone such irresponsible shirking of academic opportunities! We merely mention it to emphasise the high regard in which tutorials and supervisions are (rightly) held. Essentially, the tutorial/supervision system is an extraordinary privilege available only in bulk at Oxbridge. It not only allows a huge amount of information to pass between student and teacher, but also allows students to learn from each other, to express themselves coherently, and to engage in verbal debate.

The Collegiate System

The Oxford and Cambridge collegiate systems are a rare phenomenon in Britain: only Durham employs similar divisions. Whilst most British students will arrive on their first day at their new university to take their place in vast halls alongside thousands of others, or in small student flats with a couple of strangers, a new Oxbridge undergraduate will often arrive at their Porters' Lodge to be greeted by their college 'parents'; two second or third year students with immediate responsibility for their welfare, who will help them carry their belongings to their private rooms. The days and nights of the notorious 'Freshers' week' will be spent with fellow first-years from college, forging friendships that can last a lifetime. Usually these friendships last about three weeks (conventional wisdom states that you spend your second two terms getting rid of the friends you made in your first), but they still serve to cushion the blows of radically new experiences.

Individual colleges at Oxford and Cambridge enjoy a surprising degree of autonomy, controlling to some extent their own entrance policies, permanent staff, finances and disciplinary proceedings. Each college employs a body of Fellows or Dons whose research and teaching largely defines its academic reputation. The head of the College may have any one or more of a number of titles including: Master / Mistress, President, Provost, Rector, Principal, Dean and Warden. These individuals are sometimes chosen, in addition to their scholarship, for the power and influence they can exert on the college's behalf. Each college also has a large number of non-academic staff who regulate the life of the buildings and students. The most significant for the average undergraduate are the Porters, and the Bedders/Scouts. Porters, as their names suggest, are generally stationed in the college gatehouse, and are responsible for overseeing the comings and goings of students, tourists and visitors. The position of Head Porter is a venerable and authoritative role, and students do well to behave respectfully to all porters if they wish to keep out of trouble during their three or four years. Bedders at Cambridge and Scouts at Oxford clean the students' rooms. They are the first people many students see in the mornings / afternoons, and are for the most part completely unshockable, with a tendency to hoover loudly if anyone is still in bed after lunch.

Each college will support a certain number of undergraduates (usually living on College property for their first and final years) and a smaller proportion of postgraduates studying for MAs, MPhils or doctorates, who are more likely to live out. Each college has a dual function; it is the hub of pastoral life, the place where you live, eat and socialise, and also the centre of academic life. Undergraduate students will have within their college an academic 'Director of Studies' (D.O.S.) or 'Tutor' responsible for their intellectual growth as well as, at Cambridge, a tutor who is in charge of their welfare. Though your D.O.S. or tutor may not be qualified to teach you the syllabus beyond their specialist subjects, they will select the supervisors and tutors who are, and will always be the final word on all matters academic. Indeed, the only areas likely to affect you as an undergraduate student where authority is centralised in a single University-wide body are lectures and exams, both of which are orchestrated by the faculty responsible for a given subject. Colleges are also physically discrete: each has its own grounds and accommodation, which are generally walled off from the rest of the city. As a result of their physical and academic independence, each college has a strong character of its own, and a separate identity that its students are free either to embrace or ignore. The character of a college depends upon both the make-up of its students and fellows/dons, and its traditions and history, with records and stories that stretch back (in most cases) for centuries; the bursar of Corpus Christi College, Cambridge, can tell you how many gold florins (presumably compounded with four hundred years of interest) Christopher Marlowe still owes in rent.

Not only does this guarantee a unique experience for the members of each college, it creates tremendous diversity in university life as a whole: each friend you make in a new college opens up a new corner of the pocket universe, with new paintings, traditions, dinners, venues and parties. However, the greatest advantage of the collegiate system is the friendly atmosphere in which Oxbridge students conduct their day to day existence. Even the less pleasant elements of University life, such as financial discussions, take place in familiar surroundings between people living in a familial environment. Whilst college life tends to be warm and inclusive, none of the activities that bind a given college together are ever compulsory. For those who find such an atmosphere oppressive, and yearn for the freedom and anonymity afforded by a wider social context, college can simply be a place to lay your weary head after a long night on the town.

Even if your fellow students don't completely enthral you, taking just a little time to be polite and friendly to college staff can make all the difference to your time at University. A few judicious bottles of single malt given to the porters at the end of each term can earn you such invaluable information as prior warning of practice fire alarms (handy if you intend to have overnight guests...), prompt responses to exploding water mains (remember, many college buildings are older than America) and a steady supply of spare light bulbs and printing paper that will be the envy of those students who have failed to forge amicable relationships with the right people. Broadly speaking, the collegiate system offers all the care and individual attention of a tiny establishment, with the resources and academic clout of a huge one. Most of your dealings take place face to face with people who, even if you don't know them personally, are far from strangers, and your programme of study and living arrangements can flex to accommodate your individual needs and even preferences. At the same time, if you want access to the largest libraries, the widest array of specialists, or simply a large number of people your age, then the university steps neatly into the place of your college to satisfy your requirements.

The Statistics

It's one thing to praise Oxbridge to the heights with anecdotal evidence and opinion, and another to demonstrate the truth of these claims empirically. Here, then, are some hard facts and figures:

- Cambridge and Oxford came first and second respectively in The Guardian's 2006 University Guide. The guide assesses teaching quality, staff-student ratios and graduate job prospects.

- Either Oxford or Cambridge has been top of The Times Good University Guide every year since it was first published in 1992. The guide takes a range of measures into account including: teaching, research, entry standards, student-staff ratio, investment in facilities, graduate job prospects and completion rates.

- After the 2001 general election, nearly half the Conservative MPs were educated at Oxbridge, compared with 16% Labour and 27% Liberal Democrat. This is remarkable considering that in any given year less than 1% of the population is Oxbridge-educated.

- In The Times Higher Education Supplement World University Rankings 2007, Cambridge and Oxford were the only UK universities featuring in the top 10, coming in at 3rd and 4th respectively. Both were placed above Stanford, Yale and Princeton in a list based on teaching, research and international reputation.

- The Bodleian Library in Oxford and the Cambridge University Library are two of only six legal deposit libraries of the British Isles.

Networking and Recruitment

Though networking is something of a dirty word in most circles, with overtones of nepotism and presentable corruption, there is no denying the opportunities that exist at Oxbridge to meet and form links with people who will be helpful to you throughout your adult life. In its crudest form, the old boy network has died a welcome death, and no modern Oxbridge graduate would ever expect to get a job or position on the basis of the pattern of his tie. However, Oxbridge remains an important recruiting ground for many notoriously inaccessible professions, from the media to the Secret Service. Several academics are rumoured to be scouts for MI5 and MI6, and many a promising undergraduate has found himself taken out for a drink, and asked if he would like to serve his country. Sometimes, the degree to which an Oxbridge background shadows an alumnus through the course of his or her adulthood can pass out of the realms of the useful into the downright irritating: one cautionary tale tells of an Oxford graduate who came to despair of his professional life in London, and travelled to India in search of enlightenment. After several weeks he came to the foothills of the Himalayas, where he climbed the thousand stone stairs that led to an isolated Buddhist monastery. As he reached the top in exhaustion and exultation, he saw the abbot waiting for him like a vision of peace in orange robes. The venerable old man took his hand, and with a brisk shake asked, 'Keble, 1964. Am I right?'

The story has a slightly dubious provenance, but it nonetheless illustrates an important point. When talented individuals with common ambitions congregate in a single location for three of their formative years, it is almost inevitable that useful relationships will form. These can range from the kind

of political alliances that are still visibly and invisibly operating in today's government, to useful advice and contacts, or simply information on when and where to apply for the best jobs.

Most importantly of all, individuals at Oxbridge often meet others who inspire them, and whose talents and dreams complement their own. The creative, business and academic partnerships that have grown out of such meetings often form the stuff of legend, so it is worth taking a brief look at their diversity and quality.

Politics

Of the last nine prime ministers, only two (James Callaghan and John Major) were not educated at Oxford. The correlation is so strong that the Oxford Union is widely known as 'Westminster's Nursery'. Oxbridge not only dominates the domestic market for national leaders, it also exports its leadership training. Bill Clinton, though he might wish to forget the heady summer of '67 in which he 'smoked but didn't inhale', attended Oxford on the Rhodes scholarship. Benazir Bhutto used the hardnosed political skill she honed as head of the Oxford Union to become the first female prime minister of Pakistan. Rajiv Ghandi similarly moved on to an electoral victory in India after his student days at Trinity, Cambridge.

Media

Charles Moore, Alistair Campbell, Jon Simpson, Edward Stourton, Jeremy Paxman, John Humphries, Nick Coleridge- individuals whose views embrace the entire political spectrum, whose functions range from writer to editor to spin doctor. Yet all these individuals, despite their marked differences, have an Oxbridge degree in common, and attest in their diversity to the strongly independent thinking that is the hallmark of an Oxbridge education.

Comedy

Whilst Oxbridge supplies many of the figures who run British establishments, it also fosters the individuals who come to satirise those establishments, and provide a foil to their more serious kin. The British Monty Pythons started their comedy careers while members of Oxford and Cambridge acting societies. The Cambridge Footlights not only produced Graham Chapman, John Cleese and Eric Idle but also Stephen Fry, Hugh Laurie, Tony Slattery and Emma Thompson. Peter Cook, during his tenure at Private Eye, filled his magazine with savage critiques of those of his contemporaries who had moved on to political prominence, just as Ian Hislop does today. Oxford also has to answer for the great hero of rom coms, Hugh Grant. Sacha Baron Cohen (Ali G's creator and alias) attended Christ's College, Cambridge. He returned after graduation as Borat, and famously managed to persuade a senior academic to agree that 'woman with brain is like donkey with violin'.

Academia

Amongst Oxbridge's most celebrated discoveries are gravity (Newton attended Cambridge in 1661) and D.N.A. The Eagle pub on Benet Street in Cambridge still bears an inscription where, in 1956, Watson and Crick raised a glass to their Nobel prize-winning discovery. On occasion the two Universities divide such prizes between them; Sir Charles Scott Sherrington (Ox) and Edgar Douglas Adrian (Cam) received the 1932 prize for their discovery of neurones. The close competition between Trinity College, Cambridge and the whole of France for counting Nobel prize-winners amongst its progeny

is well known (Trinity is currently in the lead). Technologies and theories developed by men and women educated at these two Universities shape and continue to refine many different aspects of modern life.

Fantasy

If you have ever been led down the rabbit hole, through the looking glass, up Shelob's Tunnel on your way to Mount Doom or through the back of the wardrobe into Narnia, then you owe a couple of hours of blissful absorption to Oxbridge. Oxford and Cambridge do not only produce the Marlowes, Byrons and Miltons of this world- though they have given us such luminaries in abundance- J.R.R. Tolkien, Lewis Carol and C.S. Lewis were also at Oxford. Seeing a student in a white nightgown running across Peck Quad lawn reputedly gave the inspiration for the opening of Alice in Wonderland, and Tolkien and Lewis used to read aloud from their works in a little pub called the Eagle and Child, where their literary group, 'The Inklings', held regular meetings.

Similar accounts could be given of the record of Oxbridge graduates in the fields of engineering, espionage, architecture, art and criticism. The legal, banking and medical professions each receive a steady influx of graduates. Sometimes, the extent to which Oxbridge graduates dominate the most prestigious professions can induce criticism, and accusations of educational oligarchies. In an article in The Lawyer, for example, three of the Magic Circle firms were revealed as having 58% (Slaughter and May), 51% (Freshfields) and 44% (Linklaters) of partners from an Oxbridge background. Representatives of the largest and most prestigious companies still rely on the 'milkround' for part of their recruitment. If you look upon university exclusively as a link to a lucrative job, then Oxbridge is still one of the very best choices. Although The Times Good University Guide places Cambridge and Oxford graduates only sixth and seventh respectively on Average Starting Salaries, this may be explained by the facts that a higher proportion of Oxbridge students go on to further study and that most of the institutions that outstrip on this metric provide a primarily professional training in Medicine, Economics or Law.

Not only can an Oxbridge education open doors after university, it enables students to experience a range of different professions whilst still there. There are opportunities at both institutions to participate at an extremely high amateur level in journalism, the arts or sport. Many of the alumni mentioned above had their first experiences in their chosen field at Oxbridge, and certain specific posts (president of the Oxford Union, for example) are seen as incubators for future positions in government. A supportive atmosphere of mutual encouragement gives students the confidence to try new activities, whilst the competitive edge among their contemporaries drives them to excel. Even if they're not followed up to professional level, many graduates find that it is their hobbies and outside interests rather than their career aspirations or academic achievements, that provide the meat for future interviews.

Ultimately, the importance of the contacts each person makes at Oxbridge will depend on their chosen career or lifestyle. The importance of the friends they make, however, is a constant. Though the teaching staff and facilities at Oxbridge are excellent, there are a few other Russell Group universities that compare in terms of pure academic muscle (within the boundaries of their specialist areas, for example L.S.E. for Politics), and quality of research. It is the chance to mix with such a diverse and exceptional group of contemporaries that really makes the Oxbridge experience unique, and the inspiration and support that each individual can find among the student body is without equal.

Funding

A survey conducted by The Guardian discovered that, of the 120 universities questioned, two thirds (including Oxford and Cambridge) planned to charge the maximum £3,000 in fees for the academic year 2006-7[1]. At Oxford, bursaries of £10,000 over three years are being touted to fund students from disadvantaged backgrounds (Dr John Hood - Vice Chancellor of Oxford University - has claimed that these non-academic 'Oxford Opportunities Bursaries' will eventually fund twenty percent of students), whilst Cambridge's equivalent is a £3,000 a year bursary scheme.

At a meeting of CMU (Campaigning for Mainstream Universities, the body representing post-92 universities), the vice-chancellor of Middlesex blasted what he called the 'resources apartheid' which saw Oxford and Cambridge achieving an annual turnover of £650 million each to cover their 17,500 students, whilst Middlesex was expected to cope on £125 million for its 22,000. At the same time, despite this vast turnover, Oxbridge accounts are heavily in the red; Oxford makes a £9,000 loss on each student from within the E.U. that walks through its gates, and Cambridge's annual losses are only sustainable thanks to the income from its exam board.

The truth is that, whatever their current financial situation, no talented student will ever be turned away from Oxbridge due to a lack of sufficient funding. As

[1] Guardian Education, Jan 6th 2005

well as the bursaries mentioned above to cover tuition fees (which are not themselves payable up-front, but repayable as instalments once an £18,000 threshold has been crossed in postgraduate earnings), individual colleges have a vast safety net of hardship grants, bursaries and scholarships designed to catch any students who fall off the financial high-wire.

It is not only the financially disadvantaged who benefit from Oxbridge funding policies. The loss made by Oxford on each student hints at the extent to which student life at all levels is subsidised; not only the academic process itself, but living expenses are heavily shored up by colleges, a large proportion of whom provide on-site cafeteria, accommodation and even bar facilities throughout your course of study.

Though funding can be somewhat college-specific-Trinity (Cam), for example, can offer its students a range of bursaries and scholarships that less wealthy colleges could not- it can be taken as a general rule that, even factoring in the cost of living in the cities of Oxford and Cambridge (higher than in some other large university towns) a prudent student will leave Oxbridge in a better financial condition than an equivalent graduate from almost anywhere else in the country, notwithstanding their high post-graduate earnings.

A Hundred Ways to Spend an Afternoon

During the Michaelmas (Winter) and Lent/Hilary (Spring) terms, when everyone is relatively free from the immediate pressure of exams (though Oxfordians will always face those pesky Termly exams called 'Collections'), the atmosphere of both Oxford and Cambridge can resemble a sort of mini-renaissance. It would be quite possible over the eight weeks for a fanatically devoted student to see a sporting event in the afternoon, a concert or debate in the evening, and a new play or comedy routine at night every day without ever attending the same event twice. Some of these activities take place on a university level, and some of them are college based- King's College, Cambridge, for example, is always in need of an organist or two, whilst Corpus Christi permanently requires a budding thespian to master The Playroom. A handful of the musical and sporting requirements will be filled either by scholarships (as with the King's choral awards) or by the arrangements of admissions tutors (as with the small number of giant Canadian fullbacks in their late twenties who turn up to do suspiciously vague MAs). The vast majority of all other extra-curricular functions and positions, however, including the most prestigious such as President of the Oxford Union, are filled by rank and file students. Many of these will have had no previous experience in their future area of non-academic interest before they attended: one of the best features of Oxbridge is the opportunity to discover, perhaps for the first time, the particular passion that will motivate you for the rest of your life

Failing that, you can cross-dress and sing cabaret songs for a few weeks, or don lycra and hone your physique in a boat on the Isis or the Cam. Usefully, the sheer range of activities that keep Oxbridge life vital and stimulating means that it does not really matter what particular pursuits you think might interest you. To continue to function, Oxbridge simply needs people with interests outside their chosen degree course. In addition to all the drinking, political and sporting societies jostling for your time and attention, here is a brief list of a few of the more esoteric options which you may like to consider:

- The Giant Vegetable Society- A society devoted to the exclusive purpose of growing vegetables of prodigious size.

- The Booty Crew- A group of students who have sworn to propagate hip hop, peace and urban music at all costs through the organisation of regular parties.

- The Assassins- The legendary social club now banned at Oxford whose initiation process is shrouded in mystery, but allegedly has a statistical probability of survival.

- The Piers Gaveston- Social club formerly patronised by Hugh Grant where everybody goes and parties naked in a field.

- The Anarchists Society- A political group with famously disorganised meetings.

- The Trinity Nightclimbers- A reputedly defunct body of students who would scale the walls and roofs of the buildings of Oxbridge by moonlight.

Improving chances before the interview

Choosing the Right Course

Perhaps the most fundamental decision each prospective candidate must make is which course to study. Choosing the right course for you not only ensures you will get the most from your time at university, it can also maximise your chance of making a successful application. Ultimately no-one can make this decision for you (and they shouldn't try, not even if Dad and Granddad read Law at Clare in '76 and '46 respectively) but the following general advice will help you to make an informed decision.

One of the most common queries is, 'Should I choose the subject in which I get the best marks, or the one that interests me the most?' When answering this, you should consider the fact that you will be studying your subject exclusively for three or four years. Any short-term benefits you might derive from being quicker in that discipline than you would have been in another will quickly evaporate, as constantly battling against your proclivities will erode the quality of your work. Conversely, a real love for a subject will often more than compensate for an initial lack of skill. Thus it is usually better to choose your passion over your forte (if they are not one and the same). However, bear in mind that many AAB offers specify an A in the chosen subject- if there is such a large discrepancy between your academic abilities that you risk not attaining your offer by choosing your passion, you may be forced to reconsider whether Oxbridge is the right place for you to study your chosen subject.

If you are considering a degree that will lead to a professional qualification (such as Medicine or Law) you should only apply if you feel absolutely certain of your choice. Not only do these courses tend to be among the most competitive, they also test your total commitment at the interview. Many candidates feel compelled to apply for these courses because they fear that, if they do not, they will miss out on the option of these careers forever. If you feel this pressure, you should remember that a Law conversion course only takes one year longer than the equivalent qualification for a Law student, and that magic circle firms take approximately a third of their trainees from non-Law backgrounds. There is also a graduate fast track programme for Medicine, reducing the five year training to four years for those with Science A-levels. Thus if you are unsure at the age of 17 how you would like to spend the rest of your professional life, it is probably better not to leap into a course prematurely.

Finally, there is the dangerous and exciting option of choosing an unknown subject. Subjects not directly leading on from A-Level courses tend to be less heavily subscribed than the courses that are obvious extensions of ideas encountered in the classroom, precisely because they are unknown quantities. If there is a particular language, culture or historical period to which you have found yourself drawn in your extra-curricular life, then you may wish to pursue them in Egyptology or Anglo-Saxon, Norse & Celtic. Passionate interest is usually the best possible basis for a degree, and no candidate will be disadvantaged at interview by not having a ready-made academic grounding.

Interviewers will be looking for keen amateurs. Anyone applying speculatively for such courses, either because they feel they will be easier to get into or because they see them as a good career move (for example future business men and women wanting to learn Chinese) should consider that specialist courses tend to attract highly impassioned competition, and that the usual levels of dedication necessary for an enjoyable period of study will need to be exceptionally high in tiny faculties with specific and highly esoteric programmes.

Even after you know what it is you want to do, you must choose the way in which you wish to do it. When making their applications, candidates should be aware of the subtle distinctions between a subject and a course. A student taking Geography at Cambridge, for example, will have far less need for Wellingtons and Kendal Mint Cake than a student at Oxford, where a first year field trip is compulsory.

Overleaf are details of two popular courses at Oxford and Cambridge, one a Humanity and one a Science, giving information on the admissions criteria, structure and particular slant of the course, and the differences between them at the two institutions.

Though there are important differences between the ways in which each subject is approached at each institution, there are far more extreme examples of divergence in other subject areas that represent fundamentally different ways of thinking about certain subjects and how they should be taught. One such comparison can be made between Natural Sciences (Physical) at Cambridge and its nearest equivalents at Oxford, Physics and Chemistry. The philosophy behind the method of the former dictates that a broad grounding in a range of disciplines gives candidates more scope and that the knowledge they acquire will

	Cambridge	Oxford
Course	History	History (Modern)
Admissions	Submission work will be requested if called to interview with further written tests at some colleges. No H.A.T. No joint honours, though sheer scope of the course and option to 'borrow' papers from other disciplines effectively amounts to the same thing, particularly in Politics and Classics.	History Aptitude Test (H.A.T.) sat before interview. May be taken as joint honours with Modern Languages, History (Ancient), Economics, English or Politics. Those called for interview will be asked to send an essay on a historical topic.
Course Content & Structure	1st / 2nd year s - Part I: selection of five papers from a possible list of 22 with choice from the B.C. era up to modern times. There is a compulsory extended essay investigating a theme in comparative history. 3rd year - 5 Units; a general paper on Historical Argument and practice, and four other papers chosen from 40 options which span the centuries and continents. There is the option to write a dissertation.	1st year - Four compulsory courses, History of the British Isles, General History, Historical Methods and Optional Paper. You are required to pass first year Mods (exams). 2nd / 3rd years - 6 subjects are taken; British History, General History, Disciplines of History and a thesis are compulsory. Then through the 'further subject' and 'special subject' papers (specific in time and place), there is the option to study almost anything.

complement and help to develop their specialism. At Oxford, meanwhile, an official blurring of the disciplines is frowned upon, as immediate and exclusive engagement with one branch of study is seen as more efficient and ultimately more effective in producing good scientists. Knowing exactly what a course involves is thus far more than a sot thrown to your interviewer to convince them of your commitment- it is an essential step on the way to figuring out what direction you want your intellectual development to take.

	Cambridge	Oxford
Course	Natural Sciences (Physical). 3 or 4 year degree. Not joint honours but range of options effectively amounts to the same thing. You can for example focus on maths, or take biological sciences or computer science options. Those wishing to study Chemical Engineering in their second year can take Natural Sciences in their first year.	Physics (Chemistry may also be taken independently). 3 year BA Physics Hons degree. 4 year MPhys Physics degree. Joint honours possible with Philosophy.
Admissions	You must have two of Maths, Physics, Chemistry and Biology at A level. Almost half of the colleges require you to take the TSA at interview. If you were to read Maths with Physics you would be required to take the Maths STEP paper.	There is a written exam at interview. Applicants must have Maths and Physics A-level.
1st Year	Part 1A of Tripos. You read 3 experimental sciences and a course in mathematics. You gain a very broad scientific grounding.	There are four compulsory written papers and one short option paper where you can choose between astronomy, complex ideas and quantum ideas. Exams (Prelims) at the end of this year.
2nd Year	Part 1B of Tripos, allowing further specialisation in 3 subjects for those who have taken the appropriate 1A courses (Mathematics and Physics, for example, will qualify a student to do Advanced Physics). Admission to the fourth year is dependent on performance in 2nd year exams.	You take finals in part A of your degree. Like the first year you must study the core courses which range from Thermal Physics to Mathematical methods, and there is another Short Option paper. Exams are also dependent on satisfactory lab work. At the end of your 2nd year you must decide whether to take the 3 or 4 year course.
3rd Year	Part II. You continue with your part 1B subjects and have the option take up a new subject. You have the opportunity to gain highly specialised knowledge and research experience. Most students undertake a research project. Those who wish to stay on for a fourth year tend to specialise at this point.	MPhys Part B - 3 written papers on the core modules and a short option paper. BA Part B - 2 written papers on the core modules, a short option paper and a project
4th Year (optional)	Part III Most students stay on for a fourth year, graduating with a Masters in Natural Sciences and an additional B.A. Course now begins to come close to the boundaries of modern research, so the teaching is structured around specialisation in, for example, Particle Physics, Astrophysics or Semi Conductor Physics.	Part C of the MPhys consists of a project and then preparation for two major option papers and the major options include astrophysics, laser sciences, particle physics, theoretical physics, physics of atmosphere and oceans and condensed matter physics.

As can be seen from these examples, the difference in course structure is fundamental. Oxford Physicists get an earlier induction into their chosen subject, but Cambridge Natural Scientists may get a wider view of the available options before settling on one subject, and gain a broader base for their scientific knowledge through the inclusion of elements of the chemistry syllabus.

Choosing the Right College

There are several factors that should assist in a sensible choice of college:

- **Does the college offer my course?**
- **Is the college located centrally?**
- **How big is the college?**
- **How rich is the college?**
- **How academic is the college?**
- **How likely am I to get in?**

Whilst some of these questions might seem superficial or even inappropriate, their effect on your Oxbridge experience can be quite pronounced. A rich, large college, for example, may be in a better position to provide you with three years of accommodation, which may itself be heavily subsidised, dramatically reducing not only your living costs but the time and effort you have to put in to sorting out your domestic arrangements. The centrality of your college will define the degree to which you socialise with others in the city centres or lounge at the cosy fireside of collegiate life (almost all colleges have their own bar and Junior Common Room) The size may determine the atmosphere: friendly but a little claustrophobic in smaller colleges, intimidating but more diverse in the larger ones. The distance of your college relative to your faculty can also have a disproportionate effect on your attendance at lectures, and, if local lore is to be believed, on the size of your thighs (reaching some colleges by bicycle can be the student equivalent of the Tour de France...)

For most people the last question is likely to be the most significant: how likely am I to get in? The ratio of successful to unsuccessful applications can vary as dramatically from college to college as it can from subject to subject. The strategic combination of less heavily-subscribed degree courses with less popular colleges can maximise your chances. Thus a pupil applying for certain subjects at the all-female Oxbridge Colleges will be considerably more likely to make a successful application - certainly for their first choice college - than a pupil of similar ability applying for Medicine at, say, Christ Church, Oxford. As a general rule, the higher the academic reputation of the college, the harder it will be to secure a place.

Coupled with the varying degrees of competition, there is the political character of the college to consider, with certain institutions traditionally admitting different proportions of maintained and public school pupils. It is a stated policy of Cambridge (and the same principle can be applied to Oxford) to 'ensure that, as far as possible, an applicant's chance of admission to Cambridge does not depend on choice of college'. Whilst this is a worthy aim, the statistics would suggest it remains as yet unrealised. There is also the pooling system to contend with (see below).

It would be unfair to single out individual colleges and individual cases, but it has been known for certain colleges to have a higher proportion of students from a given background than others. It is important to state, however, that these tendencies are never a matter of policy, and a quality candidate from a background not shared by the vast majority of that college's intake will never be turned away on principle. It is also the case that, at a time when the admissions process is coming under particular political scrutiny, many colleges are actively seeking to recruit outside of their usual pool of applicants, and to increase diversity within their student body. It is not the intention of this book to suggest at any point that a certain 'type' of person will be more likely to get into Oxbridge than another. Such an inference would be as unhelpful as it would be untrue. Amongst the student body, the kinds of distinctions that make up the following statistics tend to melt into irrelevance within the first few days of first year anyway. However, it is worth bearing certain factors in mind for the purposes of application, if only with a view to deciding where you are most likely to fit in.

It is also possible to make an open application. If there is no college which you would prefer not to attend, then this can be a smart move. However, there are very few people who will not, with a little research, develop certain college preferences, some of which will not be too competitive. Thus, whilst an open application can shift part of the work onto Oxbridge, testing your ambivalence with a little investigation of your own is highly recommended.

However, it need not be the defining feature of your Oxbridge experience- all lectures are centrally determined by the faculty, as are final exams, and though your college can provide a stable base of friendships, many students prefer to orientate their social life towards the clubs, pubs and societies of the cities. Students tend to be as involved or as distant from college life as their tastes dictate. This is particularly true of larger colleges, where the sheer size of the student body prohibits the formation of the kind of close, inclusive communities found in smaller colleges.

N.B. In recent years Oxford has moved towards a centralised admissions system where you apply to the University rather than an individual college. Although at present most applicants still nominate a college, 15% now simply make an open application. Students making an open application have the same success rate as those who specify a college, and if you find the prospect of choosing somewhere daunting or confusing then this can be an excellent option.

The Pooling System

The pooling system exists in different forms at both Oxford and Cambridge, and though a candidate will only encounter it post-interview (if at all), it is worth mentioning in this section because it may affect your choice of college, and may precede a second round of interviews.

The tendency is to consider pooling as the poor cousin of acceptance or even a diluted form of rejection, but this is simply not the case. Colleges pool candidates for one reason: they have had an exceptionally strong series of interviewees for a very limited number of places, and they feel another college could benefit from seeing those to whom they have not been able to offer places. This is by no means an odd way to enter the universities. In 2006 at Cambridge, for example, 714 of the 2,879 candidates who were placed in the Winter Pool were made offers, of which 127 were offered a place by the college that pooled them in the first instance. Nor are you inevitably pooled to a less popular college. Admittedly it is unlikely anyone would be pooled to Trinity (Cam) for Maths or St John's (Ox) for English, but the random quality and quantity of applicants in any given year means that anyone can end up pretty much anywhere. If you are pooled and asked for interview at another college, a simple glance at the second college's website should be more than sufficient additional preparation. Interest in the course is far more important than interest in the individual institutions.

At Oxford, there are specific pooling units for certain subjects. Thus applicants for a given subject to a given college may find themselves pooled to a listed number of other colleges. There are several pooling units, each comprising about ten colleges. It is worth checking in the prospectus which colleges you might end up interviewing with if your primary college decides to pool you. If you have a strong aversion to the Greyfriar's monks, or were once caught on CCTV doing something unfortunate in the Balliol quad, you might want to check that there is no chance you will be pooled and subsequently suffer preaching/identification.

Another quirk of the Oxford system is the making of 'Pool' (or 'open') offers. These are firm conditional offers that guarantee a university place (provided you get the grades) but make no promises as to which college you will attend. This is designed to prevent talented individuals from slipping between the cracks in the collegiate system.

Cambridge has a different approach, operating a Winter Pool (by far the most common) and a Summer Pool (rarer, and dealing exclusively with applicants who already have their A-level results). The Winter

Pool, as at Oxford, consists of candidates of a high quality looking to get offers at colleges other than their first choice. During the Summer Pool, colleges reassess those of their candidates who did not get their required grades, and make unconditional offers to a handful of students who already have their A-level results.

There is a limited amount of information you need to know about the pooling system, as the bureaucratic machinery will kick in and guide you through the process if needs be. The main thing to remember is that pooling does not make you a second-class interviewee, and that the system is in place to make the admissions process that bit fairer.

Personal Statement

Though still not as influential a tool as it is in the American system, the importance of the personal statement has increased tremendously in recent years as a result of the large number of candidates predicted top A-Level grades. It is quite possibly the most significant single feature of your application (after the interview itself), and it is also the first piece of written work on which your prospective tutor can judge your abilities.

Your personal statement should be viewed in context- it will appear on an admissions tutor's desk among hundreds of similar documents, all of them representing strong students with at least AAB grade predictions. To secure you an interview, it has to leave him or her convinced that you posses those extra qualities of intelligence and academic commitment that set you apart from the others. Moreover, it should give the impression that you will be an interesting and amicable person with whom to spend the next three or four years. To put it another way, this is the main window through which your potential interviewer may glimpse the bounteous garden of your mind before December. It is your job to tempt them inside; make sure it is well kempt, fruitful, varied and fertile.

Though there are no hard and fast rules as to how to structure a personal statement, a good basic template is:

1st Paragraph

An introduction to why you feel compelled to study your given subject, and why that discipline is significant and inspiring. As your personal statement goes out to several prospective universities, you cannot give an account of why you are applying for that course at Oxford or Cambridge. A quote from a historical figure or personal hero can make the perfect ice breaker to defuse Personal Statement awkwardness, but if you do go for a quote make sure you understand its relevance.

2nd Paragraph

An account of the specific areas of interest you have within a given discipline, and the extra-curricular activities you have undertaken in pursuit of a greater understanding of your subject. Any trips, books, or experiences you found particularly inspiring, and why. Why does your particular area of interest in this subject make you well suited to the course? For example, an applicant might mention their school trip to Hastings, and how this gave them a genuine sense of the importance of history as a 'real life' phenomenon: something that exists outside of the pages of a

textbook. An outstanding candidate might go on to add that for them, this is part of the attraction to a teaching method that places particular emphasis upon the use of first-hand original source material. Paragraphs 1 and 2 together should occupy about three quarters of the total statement.

3rd Paragraph

Here the focus can shift slightly from the academic to the personal. Cover extra-curricular activities not related to your course, and give the reader a glimpse of the kind of person you are outside of the classroom. If you get the place, your admissions tutor is going to have to live with you. Your behaviour will reflect on the reputation of your college. Bear this in mind, and show yourself in your best light.

4th Paragraph

A link back into your choice of course. Tie off the personal statement with a one or two line reminder of why you want to study your subject.

Have your teachers, your parents and friends read and reread your personal statement for you. Broadly speaking, you should come across as likeable, interesting, intelligent and passionate about your subject. Finally, when it's done, leave it alone! Many a promising personal statement has been spoiled by excessive tinkering.

The rest of this chapter covers these points in more detail, and sheds some light on the more obscure aspects of the personal statement to help you to tackle your first draft.

Your Subject and What It Means to You

When considering how to begin, honesty really is the best policy. Try to think about what it is that fascinates you about your chosen discipline, and why you think it is worthy of three, four or more years of study. If you have ever come across a quote or phrase which perfectly distils and expresses your feelings, you may want to employ it. An aspiring Physicist, for example, might begin with Einstein's assertion that 'God does not play dice with the universe', and then go on to say how the capacity to understand and deconstruct the world around us through accurate mathematical formulae is what truly draws them to Physics (or Natural Sciences (Physical) depending on your choice of University). They might then say what part of the course or subject it was that epitomised this fascination.

Subject-Related Extra-Curricular Activities

It is not enough when writing the UCAS form simply to mention the parts of your course that you have found fascinating, though this is a good start. Again, when considering which areas of your subject to single out for special attention, picture your application in context: your prospective History tutor may get 30 different Personal Statements citing an interest in Nazi Germany or the English Civil War, and the one that focuses instead on the Opium Wars is likely to look more intriguing, at least at first glance. Successful Oxbridge candidates are those who have gone beyond the boundaries of their course, and accumulated an idiosyncratic series of subject-related interests.

The reasons for listing extra curricular activities relating directly to your subject are less opaque than those relating to their non-course-related counterparts. Cambridge courses, particularly in the humanities, require a high degree of intellectual autonomy. Courses in English and Philosophy particularly need a lot of outside reading in order to get the best from the lectures and supervisions/tutorials. The ideal approach is to show how some particular idea or area of study within your recent studies inspired you to explore more on that subject in your own time, developing a curricular interest into a personal passion. Any applicant who can take advantage of the UCAS form to demonstrate this kind of faculty will stand a better chance of being asked for interview, and will be at a distinct advantage throughout the selection process. More importantly, strong candidates will be taking such measures for themselves rather than to impress any individual or institution with a glittering UCAS Form.

Unlike other extra-curricular activities, there is a good chance that the things you list in relation to your course will be raised during the interview proper. It is therefore imperative that any given hobby or special area of interest is genuine and well researched. Giving any special area of expertise is effectively inviting your interviewer to question you on it; remember, they are trying to give you an opportunity to show yourself in your best light. If you wrote something down in a panic because it sounded good, and then forgot to research it, you could (and, frankly, should!) find yourself in trouble.

You should aim to introduce subject related activities in the second paragraph of your personal statement, developing on from the more general engagement with your chosen subject laid out in the first paragraph.

There can be no definitive list of activities that will necessarily lead to a successful application. The following, however, are some activities that some of our clients over the years have put: membership of local or national science clubs, attendance or volunteer work at hospitals, theatres, museums, exhibitions, historical sites, relevant trips abroad (not your summer holiday in Tenerife), extra reading, with the titles and authors of the works, involvement with literature/arts societies.

Subject-Related Extra-Curricular Activities: Summary

Should:

- Be mentioned in the second paragraph of the personal statement
- Be things that genuinely inspire you
- Be well researched
- Sustain relatively extensive conversation
- Where appropriate, derive from an area studied in school which inspired you to further action

Should NOT:

- Be made up (none of your friends believe you spent your holidays as a photojournalist in Iraq, and neither will your interviewer)
- Consist exclusively of work that was covered in class

Extra-Curricular Activities

A brief disclaimer

When in 2003 the sociologist and mother of a successful applicant Elfi Pallis published her book 'Oxbridge Entrance - The Real Rules', she received mixed comments. One of the principle objections to her advice, issued as a structured rebuttal by Geoff Parks, the Director of Admissions for Cambridge Colleges, was the unwarranted emphasis she placed on extra-curricular activities. Citing this as a point where 'the advice offered slips from the misleading into the positively unhelpful', Parks goes on to say how the idea that successful applicants demonstrate on their personal statements evidence of 'voluntary work', 'sport', 'musical ability' and 'leadership roles' is completely unfounded. 'We regularly advise applicants that if, in apportioning their time, they have to choose between exploring their chosen subject in greater depth or acquiring more C.V. points, we would rather they opt for the former than the latter'. You must remember when constructing your personal statement that the criteria for judgement are extremely narrow and simple. Academic commitment and ability are all.

Having offered this caveat, it is worth touching on why a personal statement should include information on extra-curricular activities at all. Though they will never form the criteria for selection, they can offer a number of helpful opportunities if well deployed. They can help tutors to distinguish between the vast sheaves of applications which land on their desks come interview time. If an individual comes across through their extra-curricular pursuits as well-rounded and interesting, it cannot damage their chances and, in some isolated cases where there has been a shared passion, discussion of these hobbies has been known to occupy a sizeable chunk of the interview! Secondly, it can prove a good angle to mention in relation to choice of college. If, for example, your chosen destination has a strong reputation in a particular sport or art, you can cite this as one of the reasons why you made your application there. Thirdly, it's relatively important that your prospective tutor/supervisor will be able to get on with you well. As discussed above, the Oxbridge teaching system is highly personal and, though no academic would choose a likeable idiot over a cantankerous genius, somewhere at the back of their minds may linger the question 'Can I sit for an hour a week in a small room with this person for three years?'

Bearing these ideas in mind, but recognising also that extra-curricular activities pale into insignificance when compared to their subject-related kin, here are a few of the things our candidates have done, followed by extracts to give an idea of good and bad practice.

- Any interest in other cultures, languages or religions
- Archaeology
- Arts
- Astronomy
- Attendee or head of any society
- Charity work or community service (though not as part of a court order!)
- Drama: Costume design, Stagehand
- Duke of Edinburgh Award
- Film
- Mentoring schemes
- Music
- Political involvement
- Prefect
- School journalism or editorial work
- Sports (anything from polo to pool to petanque)
- Travel
- Website design
- Work experience
- Young Enterprise

Examples

[Third paragraph of the personal statement]

Pupil 1

'In my spare time, I play netball for the school team, and run cross country. I recently completed the London Marathon, gaining sponsorship for the Royal Marsden Hospital. I have a passion for historical fiction, particularly books set in ancient Rome and Greece. I also grow bonsai trees, which has stimulated me to begin to look into Japanese culture.'

This candidate has produced a good account of her extra curricular activities. Space is used efficiently, with the Marathon illustrating both charitable enterprise and physical prowess. Playing netball for the school team shows an ability to function socially with peers. The comments on historical fiction and bonsai trees both demonstrate an open mind that identifies an area of interest, and then independently seeks out further information. Finally, she has come across as an individual, someone it would be interesting to chat to for half an hour, and her application will be less likely to be forgotten in the pile of hundreds.

Pupil 2

'Finally, one of my motivating passions is drama. I played the lead in the school play, which was Harold Pinter's 'The Caretaker', I also played the part of Puck in 'A Midsummer Night's Dream', and I went to see 'Troilus and Cressida' at The National Theatre as part of my Theatre Studies Course. I also greatly enjoy sports, reading and doing charity work.'

This student has wasted space and reduced impact by

simply listing every play he has done in his time at school. His citing of the trip to The National Theatre is not extra-curricular, it was part of his course- this implies he does not have enough real interests outside of his course to fill up six lines. He has given no details of which sports or books he likes, how he feels they have interested him, or how he would like to pursue them in the future, making him far less memorable than other applicants.

Extra-Curricular Activities: Summary

Should:

- Be mentioned in the third paragraph of the UCAS statement
- Include the activities and achievements of which you are particularly proud
- If the need arises, sustain five minutes of interesting conversation
- If at all possible, be suited to the activities your chosen college offers
- Give a sense of who you are
- Where possible, touch on how you feel this pursuit has developed your character

Should NOT:

- Occupy more than about a fifth of the total personal statement
- Be an unedited account of everything you have ever done
- Be fictitious
- Make you sound like a child or a lunatic - Pokemon and dwarf tossing each have their own attractions, but are probably best not mentioned until well after matriculation, if at all

2

Submitting Written Work

Some colleges, when issuing an invitation to interview, will request the submission of written work, particularly for the Humanities and Languages. Though the requests will specify exactly what is to be submitted, the general rule is two recent essays written in class in the normal course of the curriculum.

When choosing the essays, choose work that shows you naturally and in your best light. Interviewers will immediately see through something that is either a) specially produced for the occasion b) the product of six months exhaustive research or c) downloaded from Sparknotes. Flout the specific request for work produced in the normal course of study at your own risk. However, that is not to say that, when choosing an essay, you cannot undertake some small rewrites and corrections. Go through a piece of work with a teacher, parent or tutor, correct any silly mistakes, expand on the best points and edit out the weakest, and then ask a teacher to remark it. This will ensure that the pieces you send in have the unmistakeable whiff of authenticity, but don't stink. The pieces you choose should be as recent as possible to show the current state of your intellect, and also to ensure that, if an interviewer wants to discuss some of the issues you address, they will be fresh in your mind.

Also, once you have taken the decision to apply, bear in mind that any essay set in class could potentially be the one you choose to send off- if a topic fascinates you or you know it well then put that bit of extra effort in to make it a really worthy piece of work.

Getting to Know Your Interviewer

Whilst your college may not reveal who will be taking your interviews until the day you arrive at the

Porter's Lodge, it is likely that you will be meeting the most senior academic in your subject at your chosen college, and possibly several of their subordinates. A quick glance at the college website will give you a profile of each tutor, and introduce their particular field of specialisation. It will also usually list their published research. Dropping their name into Google will give you further access to any articles or shorter pieces they have written, together with any open lectures they might be giving in Cambridge, Oxford or elsewhere.

Once you have this information, it is up to you whether you want to make use of it. It would be a waste of time to read the entire opus of your prospective interviewer (and you might do so only to arrive at the college and discover they are off for the week with 'flu!), and you would be wise to remember the old playground rule- no-one likes a suck-up. In the sciences, it is unlikely you would have the necessary grounding at this stage to understand any of his or her research. There are, however, a few sensible things you can do. You might brush up on the part of your syllabus that pertains to their specialist area, or do a bit of extra curricular reading on that subject. You could also make sure you are up to date on recent developments in that area, such as newly published theories or discoveries, or news stories that have ignited debate (though again, if your future mentor is a particle physicist holding forth on sub-atomic theory, it might be better just to stick to your syllabus!). As we always advise with extra-curricular reading, and this is a theme that runs throughout this book, don't do it in order to impress anyone (parents, teachers, Oxbridge fellows, friends) - you should be doing it purely and simply because you genuinely enjoy it. A consequence of this will of course be that all of the above groups will be impressed.

Written tests

With a failing trust in A-Levels as an adequate method of differentiating academic ability amongst the upper echelons of a national cohort of 17 year-olds, Oxbridge are returning to written tests of their own in their selection of candidates. There are two externally administered standardised tests at both universities, the LNAT and the BMAT, which cover Law and Medicine respectively. In addition to these, recent years have seen the reintroduction of the STEP paper for Maths at Cambridge and the introduction of the Thinking Skills Assessment (TSA) for various subjects at Cambridge and the History Aptitude Test (HAT) for History at Oxford. There is also a smattering of written tests arranged by individual colleges for candidates to take whilst they are there for their interviews. In order to check whether or not your prospective college sets a written test at interview, look on the college website for admissions information. In the case of Cambridge, a handy table is also often available at the back of the prospectus.

General Principles

Though each written test will have its own requirements and parameters, there are two general points that may help anyone considering the written portion of the interview process.

Firstly, most of the tests and exams set at University entrance level are extremely tough. This can come as a shock to the system for students who are used to flicking on their mental cruise control and coasting through the A-Level syllabus with minimal effort. Do not judge yourself by A-Level standards- the tests have to differentiate between a far narrower band of intellectual ability than other national exams, namely pupils likely to get A or high B grades, and are therefore much harder. Accept the fact that you will be challenged and will probably get a few things wrong.

Secondly, if you are a hard and conscientious worker (and, for obvious reasons, many Oxbridge applicants are) it can be daunting to approach a test for which there is no set syllabus. The reintroduction of STEP papers and the like can be partly interpreted as a further move towards widening access, since the unfamiliarity of the material creates a level playing field on which examiners can judge candidates by their intelligence alone, and their capacity to think rather than the extent of their learning. This is not to say that outside knowledge will not be rewarded- if, for example, you find yourself writing on the legalisation of cannabis in the LNAT, and you happen to have read an article in the previous week's Economist about the cost of drug-related crime, by all means quote the source and figures. It does mean, however, that no-one can go into the exam comfortable in the fact that they know what will come up. Rather than letting this scare you, just remember that it also means there's no chance of going in and suddenly blanking as you panic and forget three months' worth of revision! Forget about knowledge, and let your confidence rest in your intelligence.

College-Specific Tests

Each college will generally set a written test for the candidates who come for interview. Most colleges will not disclose the exact nature of these tests before that time. By collating the data from the thousand or so applicants we helped in 2004, we have compiled a list of some of the different challenges you may face. This list is by no means exhaustive, and is designed to give you an idea of the kind of hurdles you might encounter, rather than to be a fixed inventory of those you will. In all cases, candidates are strongly advised to look on the University and College websites in search of sample questions, such as those to be found (at the time of writing) at:

www.maths.ox.ac.uk/prospective-students/ undergraduate/specimen-tests/index.shtml

N.B. Any historians, lawyers, vets and medics who are tempted to skip directly to the bottom of the section be warned- Oxbridge colleges have been known to set an extra hour or so of their own questions in addition to the National Aptitude Tests.

English

The English entrance test tends to be the most readily predictable of all the written tests not officially standardised across the board. The general format is an hour-long compare-and-contrast exercise between two pieces of writing, usually, but not exclusively, dramatic or poetic verse. These pieces can be derived from any period, but are often Romantic or earlier. The candidate may be invited to make an open ended comparison, but will generally find a guiding theme given in the question. This title, derived from a paper consisting of two extracts of poetry set last year at Cambridge, would be fairly typical: "Compare the attitudes of Shelley and Tate towards the relationship between words and images."

In order to prepare for this, brush up on your practical criticism skills. It can be particularly helpful to beef up your technical vocabulary by learning the terms for certain metrical patterns and poetic tricks. This will also stand you in good stead for the interviews proper; in addition to the written tests, you may be given a piece of writing before your interview to form the basis of the discussion. You will generally have about ten minutes to assess the text and come up with some good points on style, technique and meaning, ideally culminating in a guess at the period or genre from which it derives. These exercises reflect a strong bias in the Oxbridge courses towards the concrete analysis of language, and there is an unseen literature paper in Part II exams at Cambridge and one in first year Moderations exams at Oxford.

Classics and Modern and Medieval Languages

The common tendency that unites the interview experiences of ancient and modern language students applying to Oxbridge is a focus on grammar and the basic mechanisms of language, with little importance placed on either vocabulary (beyond knowing enough to give effective translations) or contemporary cultural knowledge. Remember, this is only true of the written tests, and these other features will be thoroughly discussed during the interview proper. Several of our applicants for Classics in 2004 were given one hour of Greek and one hour of Latin translation, often one in prose and one in verse. Modern linguists tended to get off more lightly, with half hour grammatical tests for their target language. To emphasise the focus on grammar, one Classics student's experience is a useful illustration: he was asked to take the Languages Aptitude Test (now in relatively frequent use at Oxford), which included finding rules for Icelandic and Akkadian verb forms, translating and forming rules for a made up language, Krempl, and writing direct speech in the style of a given article.

3

In some instances, candidates were asked for a slightly more unusual take on their subject- one applicant for Modern and Medieval Languages, for example, found herself required to write an essay in the target language on the English attitude to studying foreign cultures, as outlined in an English language article given with the paper.

Students applying for MML at Cambridge will have to tackle a single standardised test set by the University. The test takes 45 minutes, and the format consists of a written article in English from 300-350 words which candidates read and digest. There then follows a series of three questions to be answered in essay format In one of the target languages they have studied at A-Level. Markers will be looking at grammar, accuracy and self-expression. The test is both a straightforward comprehension exercise showing that you have understood the information contained in the article, and a more complex composition. Use the order of the questions to structure your essay, and focus on clarity and accuracy in answering the factual questions and linguistic range and invention in answering the more interpretive parts. Advice and a sample paper are available at:

http://www.mml.cam.ac.uk/prospectus/undergrad/applying/test.html#specimen

Broadly speaking, then, the written exams set for languages are designed to test a candidate's grip of the fundamental linguistic building blocks. Other common questions were those which asked students to make corrections to sentences, to change the tense, to switch the subject and object, to turn a noun into its verb, to shift a sentence from the positive to the negative etc. Brushing up on agreements, verb endings, tenses and so on may therefore be a more fruitful method of preparation than learning extensive lists of vocabulary, or preparing individual topics.

Mathematics, Physics and Natural Sciences (Physical)

As one candidate told us of the University-wide Oxford Physics test, she encountered 'nothing not covered in A-Level Maths,' but was asked 'to spot new things in two of the questions.' Many of the questions you are set will not involve new concepts, but will be structured in such a way as to appear new, and require the innovative application of A-Level knowledge to solve. A typical structure to these questions (be it in a written test in December or during your time at Oxbridge) is to solve a relatively simple problem and then generalise to a formula for n (see example in Chapter 7). For most of the tests encountered by our applicants there was a certain degree of choice over which questions were attempted.

As with the Language tests, the idea of the tests is to establish whether the candidate has a good grip of the basics - most tests were set without the use of calculator or tables of formulae - and to see how adept the candidate is at applying these basics to unfamiliar problems. Brush up on your mental arithmetic, try to ensure maximum coverage of the A-Level syllabus, check for sample papers on the University websites, and be prepared to apply old knowledge to new problems.

Politics, Philosophy and Economics (Oxford)

On the Hertford College website, potential P.P.E. students are given warning that the format of the test 'may vary substantially from year to year'. Whilst this is certainly the case, some broad principles can be extracted from the experiences of past candidates which may shed a little light on what to expect.

Many applicants were given a one hour written test divided into three parts that broadly encompassed the three disciplines. The first related to summarising an argument and identifying potential oversights in a value-based voting system (Politics). The second asked the candidates to differentiate between near synonyms, e.g. Justice, Fairness and Equity (Philosophy). The third had a distinctly mathematical slant, providing a cost/price spread sheet and requiring the student to work out what combination of sales would maximise profits (Economics).

In terms of preparation, work on basic arithmetic will be helpful for the Economics question. If you have taken mainly or entirely science A-Levels, bear in mind that your essay writing skills may be a little rusty, and it's worth giving them a quick polish before attempting the philosophy section, as style, structure and overall clarity will be assessed as well as content.

LNAT

The National Admissions Test for Law is comprised of one 80 minute multiple choice section, and one 40 minute essay section. Broadly speaking, the first part may be said to test your ability to process and digest the information presented in a text, and the second section to test your ability to formulate and structure coherent arguments. There is no information you can revise for the LNAT- everything you will need to answer the questions is either given on the paper, or derived from the osmotic absorption of facts and issues from the media, discussion with friends and family etc. This does not mean, however, that there is nothing you can do to practise.

Do as many sample papers as you can get your hands on. There is a sample paper on the LNAT website (**www.lnat.ac.uk**)- do NOT waste this valuable resource by peeking at the answers before you attempt it! The multiple choice section is essentially a comprehension, the grown-up version of G.C.S.E English and the baby version of the linguistic tests set by some top law firms at interview. The key to answering these is accuracy and attention to detail. The difference between getting the answer right or wrong is as likely to depend on your understanding of the question as your comprehension of the passage. Skim read the passage once, then read each question closely, and return to the section of text to which it refers for more detailed analysis. Remember that when answering these questions, you must place language under the microscope: your ability to identify assumptions, analogies, logical conclusions and objective or subjective pronouncements will depend upon the degree to which your mind can pick apart individual sentences and phrases to get at the core of their meaning. Whilst there are many different ways of reaching an answer, it can be useful to work through the five possible responses eliminating those which cannot be correct rather then searching for the right one.

For the essays, structure and coherence are all. Whereas an English, History or Classics essay might place some importance on style, in the LNAT clarity is more important than flair, and precision is more important than verbosity. Law is a Social Science, not a Humanity, and you should aim for a clinical exposition of both sides of the debate followed by a conclusion that comes down on one side. A good way to practise for this section is simply to take a list of ten controversial topics, and sketch out five points for and against in each case. One of the best patterns to establish when planning is to pay particular attention to the points on the side of the argument with which you instinctively disagree. This gets you into the habit of objective thinking and teaches you to analyse arguments on their merit. Repeatedly planning essays, and teaching yourself to generate good points on the spot, will prove more useful than writing lots of mock essays.

If you are required to sit the LNAT, we recommend that you consult Mastering the National Admissions Test for Law by Mark Shepherd, one of our consultants. Candidates are advised on how to approach both essays and multiple choice questions, and they can practise their skills on five sample tests.

HAT

The History Aptitude Test (HAT) is also divided into two parts and takes place over two hours. Candidates are advised by the rubric to spend 40 minutes reading, planning and thinking, 50-55 minutes on Section One and 25-30 minutes on Section Two. A sample paper, together with a tutor's commentary, is available on the Oxford website:

www.history.ox.ac.uk/prosundergrad/applying/hat_ introduction.htm

which provides an invaluable insight into how to formulate your responses.

Each section is based around a source given with the paper. The first section is worth 70 marks and is broken up into several questions, and the second is a 30 mark essay question. When answering both questions, there are a couple of points that candidates should keep in mind to maximise their potential. In the first section:

- Pay particular attention to the specific terms of the question.

- If you are asked to analyse a phrase or idea, pay equal attention to each part of it.

- Avoid extensive quotation from the text if you have been asked to explain a given statement.

- Use your own words, and don't just paraphrase the source.

- Concentrate on giving a critical analysis of the source, and not an account or description of its content.

- This section will also contain a question requiring you to relate the issues raised in the source to an example derived from your own historical knowledge. When answering this question, bear in mind that every fact or point you make about your chosen historical period must be strictly relevant. For example, if the question asks you to discuss a proposed relationship between economic decline and political unrest, the French Revolution might be a good period on which to focus. If, however, your analysis strays from the 'let them eat cake' side of things and the extravagances of a publicly funded monarchy into an examination of Desmoulin's trial or Robespierre's fanaticism, you will begin to lose marks. All the information must be deployed to provide a practical grounding to the theoretical argument.

In the final essay question avoid being drawn into displaying your extraneous knowledge of the period, or using the text as a point of departure to explore some other area of your interest. If it doesn't directly relate to the text, it won't get you marks. This principle works both ways - if it is a conclusion that logically derives from the given source, then it will get you marks regardless of historical reality. This does not mean that if the text raises a particular idea you should not feel free to explore it in more depth. Last year's examiners stated that, whilst candidates often made perceptive points and identified interesting problems implied by the text, they seldom pursued these through to their logical conclusions, and therefore failed to fully analyse issues that they themselves had rightly identified.

BMAT

The BioMedical Admissions Test (BMAT) consists of three discrete sections- the first is a multiple choice exam designed to test 'critical thinking'. The second is the Science- and Maths-based exam designed to test your knowledge as well as your problem-solving abilities. The third is an essay question.

Both Sections One and Two are multiple choice. There is no negative marking, and time is a tough constraint. It is therefore essential that, when facing these two papers, you do not spend too long on any individual question, and you do not leave any boxes blank at the end of the exam. Make educated guesses at any questions you are not quite sure of or do not have time to answer fully. If you come to the end of your time and there are still several unanswered questions it makes sense to tick boxes at random - you cannot decrease your score for wrong answers, and you will probably pick up a few extra marks. Never leave a question unanswered.

When answering Section One, jot down diagrams to check yourself- several of the questions set you problems which can be difficult to calculate mentally, but become clear when sketched on paper. Also, be on the look out for 'best answer' questions, as these will be unfamiliar to most candidates. 'Best answer' questions are generally text-based critical thinking problems in which all the possible options given could be correct, but only one is the most appropriate.

In Section Two, you will encounter several questions with a built-in shortcut. Spotting this shortcut will enable you to solve them in the sixty seconds or so allotted to each question. If you fail to spot it, the calculation will still be possible, but may take several minutes. It is therefore imperative that you keep your wits about you and notice all the arithmetical and mental shortcuts that are allowed by the paper; if, for example, a complicated calculation is given, but there is a hidden common denominator, spotting this will allow you to answer the question at maximum speed.

The knowledge required by Section 2 is, according to the UCLES board that sets the exam, "restricted to the equivalent of Key Stage 4 Double Science and Mathematics, but will however require an understanding level appropriate to such an able target group." Several topics included in this syllabus (such as seismic waves) are not needed for the exam (see the BMAT website, **www.bmat.org.uk**, for a list of these exceptions). Because time is short in the first two sections of the BMAT, it is essential that you not only know this information, but know it well enough to deploy it without pausing to think, scratch your head and chew the end off your pencil. Practising times tables and simple arithmetic, though it might seem a little childish, can also help you pick up speed during the exam.

Whereas Sections One and Two are both assessed by UCLES, Section 3 will be copied and sent to your prospective universities. It will be sitting on your interviewer's desk next to a copy of your personal statement, and may form part of the discussion at any interviews you have.

Your essay is the first indication of what your written work is like, unaided and under time constraints and it is therefore essential that you use this opportunity to make a good impression. Structure is all important- use a piece of scrap paper to note down all the points you wish to make, then shuffle them into logical order before beginning. If a question asks your opinion, try outlining both sides of the debate before settling on one.

The three questions on offer often cover a range of possible topics: one will usually be fact-based, whilst another might provoke a more ethical or philosophical debate. Play to your strengths when choosing your topic. The questions are usually subdivided into three parts, three mini-issues that feature in the larger debate. Use this tripartite division as a ready made structure for your answer. This will ensure clarity and logical construction of your argument.

One particularly useful piece of advice contained on the BMAT homepage regards looking forward to interview after the test is over- make sure you remember what answers you gave in Section Three, and think about areas for improvement. That way if questions over your essay arise in interview, you will be armed for discussion, and ready to mitigate any problems you may have had in the eyes of your interviewer by offering an intelligent critique of your work. It may be sensible to make a note of your answers in as much details as you can as soon as you come out of the test, so that you can remind yourself of your main arguments and prepare more details before your interview if necessary.

Good general advice and practice papers are available at **www.bmat.org.uk** and **www.ucl.ac.uk/lapt/bmat.htm.** We would also recommend that you consult Passing the UK Clinical Aptitude Test and BMAT, which was co-written by one of our consultants, Felicity Taylor. This book covers verbal, quantitative and abstract reasoning, problem solving and answering multiple choice questions. It also includes sample tests, together with explanations to help understand both correct and incorrect answers.

The interview

4

In the old days, runs the legend, when you walked into the interview the fellow threw you a rugby ball. If you dropped it, or it hit you in the face and broke your glasses, you were out. If you caught it, you were in. If you caught it and drop kicked it back, you got a scholarship.

Many of the interviews still contain some practical element, though the format has changed a little over the years. The days when Oxbridge claimed to interview every candidate who applied are over, but they still invite a very large proportion (over 90%) of those who wish to attend for interview. On the one hand this means that, provided your grades are up to scratch, you will almost certainly get a chance to impress your future instructors; on the other, so will everybody else! For this reason, the interview is the single most important factor in determining whether or not you are offered a place.

The following chapter is based on the feedback we have collated from the 30,000 applicants we have helped over the past seven years, together with factual information from the Universities themselves, advice from the ex-admissions tutors who form our Advisory Board as well as the input from our 300 Oxbridge graduates who help us carry out our various services. It covers types of interview you may receive, verbal tests, the five main qualities that a good student should demonstrate, and the things our candidates would have done differently if they had the chance again, all of which should increase your understanding of the process and help you give yourself the best possible chance of success.

How to Present Yourself

Unless specified by your college, there are no official dress requirements for the interview. Your prospective tutor or supervisor wants to see you in as relaxed a state as possible, and to get a sense of who you are, so asking everybody to wear suits would be counterproductive. That said, you should bear in mind that the interview is a formal academic occasion, and that candidates should express respect for the process and at least curb their wilder sartorial impulses.

Wear clean clothes, and avoid offensive slogans on jumpers or T-shirts. Girls can wear trousers or skirts, but if they opt for the latter they should be of a respectable length. Boys might do well to choose a long-sleeved shirt or a collared shirt and jeans (December weather in both Oxford and Cambridge makes T-shirts an unlikely choice). If you don't trust your everyday wardrobe, then you can bring along a suit and tie. Though it's seldom a requirement, you will find that many candidates feel more comfortable wearing them. If it's close to your school uniform it can also help you to get into that academic state of mind. If you are staying overnight in college accommodation you can bring a suit in your bag and decide whether or not to wear it when you see what other people have chosen.

Finally, you should remove anything that dangles, glints or jingles if you have a tendency to fiddle with it during moments of high stress. Over the course of the thousands of one-on-one mock interviews we have conducted over the past five years, we have borne witness to hundreds of favourite pieces of jewellery and locks of hair that become irresistible as the nerves set in. This can be extremely distracting - if not irritating - for an interviewer. If this is you then wear long hair up, and leave the pendant at home.

Types of Interview

In a perfect world...

A good interviewer will always be sending out signals as to when a good point has been made, when he or she would like further explanation and so on. It's the conversational equivalent of 'warmer, warmer, colder, colder...' A strong candidate will pick up on these hints and signals, and allow the interviewer to guide them towards potential answers to questions that originally appeared incomprehensible. This will be equally true of Science and Arts interviews; a Maths student may be presented with a problem which at first appears impossible, but with a series of hints and suggestions (What about rearranging the left hand side of the equation? etc.) slowly breaks down into manageable fragments. In many ways this process mirrors the technique of the tutorial/supervision. Remember, the interviewers are not setting out to fool candidates into revealing their ignorance, they are trying to help them show off their ability; they are looking to admit the best - NOT to exclude the worst. With this in mind, they are also extremely likely to question you about the topics of special interest you have put down on your UCAS form, the reasoning being that you will be at your intellectual best on material you know well. If you talk with interest and conviction about these topics, and manage to excite your interviewer's attention, you can spend a considerable portion of the interview on home turf. Finally, the tougher an interview appears to you, the better it may be going. If the interviewer has to work hard to push you to your limits, they will be led to believe that those limits are impressively distant! If you bear this in mind, something like this 'perfect world' should not be impossible.

Panel

Panel interviews are more common at Oxford than at Cambridge, but can happen at both Universities. They tend to be more intimidating than talking to one individual, and it can be harder to establish a rapport ('My school didn't warn me', recalls one Law student of her interview at Magdalene, 'and I suddenly found myself in a room with five bearded men. I felt like I'd wandered into a scene from the Old Testament.') However, the advantage is that some of the subjectivity can be eliminated from the interview process, and candidates are less likely to find themselves involved in a clash of personalities.

As a general rule, answers should be addressed to the interviewer who asked the question, with regular glances to include the other dons. It may be the case that one party leads the interview, whilst another observes and takes notes. It can be quite off-putting to have a silent presence in the room, and the observer inevitably begins to scribble furiously halfway through your response, prompting you to wonder what you have said and lose your train of thought. If one party is clearly conducting the interview whilst another watches, concentrate on forming a rapport with the speaker and be comfortable ignoring the silent presence in the corner.

Two points should also be borne in mind to help you through this potentially difficult experience. Firstly, it is our opinion as well as that of the graduate tutors we work with that ALL of these interviewers are decent people who genuinely want to see you at your best, and so will do their utmost to put you at ease. Of course it is much easier to enjoy their company with the offer of a place under one's belt but we feel that being made explicitly aware of this fact should offer some comfort. Secondly, if nerves continue to play an unwelcome part in your interview experience try to keep in mind the fact that the admissions process is,

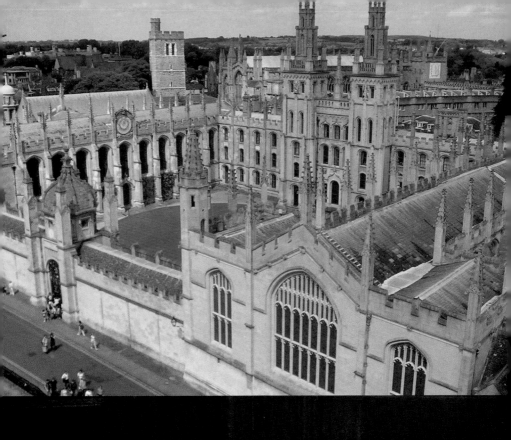

UNIVERSITY OF OXFORD

DEGREE CEREMONIES

Admission to the Sheldonian Theatre for Degree
Ceremonies is open only to the guests of those
on whom degrees are being conferred

PLEASE HAVE YOUR TICKETS READY

nonetheless, fair: every interviewee (for a given subject) is interviewed by the same people and suffering the same nerves as you.

If you feel it would be helpful to be forewarned about the format of your interview, do not hesitate to call the college admissions office and ask whether or not you should expect a panel interview.

The Aggressive, The Tough and The Rude

The aggressive interviewer may launch an intellectual assault on your beliefs, or probe your responses. They will not allow you to get away with saying something foolish, and will push you to reveal your strengths and weaknesses. Whilst an aggressive interview can feel like a gruelling experience, it gives you perhaps the best opportunity to show what you can do.

One of the most basic tactics in the aggressive interviewer's arsenal is to challenge your responses by taking an oppositional stance:

"I really struggled with the arguments against getting rid of third world debt, as I strongly feel It should be eradicated, but I guess they sussed that out."

This PPEist's experience at Oxford amply illustrates this technique. The most important thing in this case is to keep your head, and not allow your passion to cloud the analytical integrity of your responses. Remember that your interviewer may not believe the point they are arguing- it is likely they are simply playing Devil's Advocate to see how you cope with intellectual pressure. Look on it as a chance to defend your views by deploying all the evidence and theories you have in support of them, and try to strike a balance between listening to your interviewer and taking their views into account whilst maintaining and defending your own. Formulating specific opinions on issues, rather than simply dryly recounting facts or theories, is very much part of the Oxbridge ethos, and if you find yourself in a heated debate with your interviewer (so long as you remain respectful and rational) it's probably a sign that the interview is going well.

You may be asked questions which disorientate you because they appear obscure or unrelated to your subject. One of our clients registered surprise when asked 'Why don't animals have green fur?' in her Medicine interview. With such questions it is the method with which you approach the answer rather than the answer itself which is significant. A good Medic might approach this apparently bizarre question by thinking through the need for camouflage in fur colouration, the general association of green pigment in nature with chlorophyll, the limited palette of keratin and any number of other sensible points that contribute towards a response.

Throughout an aggressive interview, you should be prepared for 'Such as?' and 'For example?' questions. One of the best intellectual habits a candidate can develop in any discipline is the linking of theoretical points and conjectures to empirical data. Put simply, every time you voice an opinion, link it to an example or other evidence which supports it. If you do this effectively it will greatly reduce your chances of arguing yourself into a corner, or of saying something foolish on which your interviewer can pounce. The inverse of this is true when you are presented with data- always try to draw conclusions and base opinions on the facts before you.

Finally, remember there is always the option of backing down. If you find yourself defending the indefensible, concede the point, acknowledge the force of the interviewer's arguments and move on. Don't continue to dig a hole in the hope that blind stubbornness will look like tenacity. Remember that these

people have studied the topic under discussion for most of their adult life- there's no shame if their arguments outmatch yours, and they simply prove you wrong!

Passive

Passive interviewers may appear laid back, or friendly and garrulous. However, passive interviews are perhaps the toughest of all to negotiate, as the burden of active display falls squarely on the candidate. An aggressive or enthusiastic interviewer will drive you to perform through incisive questioning, and as you feel your mind stretched and tested you will be demonstrating the full extent of your abilities. With a passive interviewer, the onus is on you to turn the experience from a casual conversation into an intellectual discussion. You must seek to guide your interviewer towards the particular areas of your subject that interest or impassion you. You must also aim to volunteer the kinds of detailed examples a more proactive interviewer might ask you to supply in support of your ideas.

The interviewer may sit back in their chair with an inscrutable look and greet all of your responses by repeating "And then?" This variant on the passive technique can be extremely frustrating, and can lead even in the most confident candidate to the first tremors of blind panic. Take this comment from one would-be theologian-

"[The toughest question was]... either the one about whether ignorant people can know God, or how Biology and Maths aid Theology, as whatever I said, the interviewer would add 'And...?' until I got really freaked out because they don't especially!"

It is unclear from her comments whether she means that ignorant people don't especially know God, or that Maths and Biology don't especially aid Theology.

In either case, this is a classic example of a passive technique upsetting a candidate's train of thought. If you give an answer to the question and the response you get is "And...?" you are simply being invited to expand upon your ideas, or to consider the question from a different angle. Either try to develop your initial answer to its logical conclusion, or pause and reconsider the implications of the question. There may well be a particular point the interviewer hopes you will hit upon which is either just beyond the scope of your answer, or requires a different angle. If, for example, your original answer was "Biology doesn't help Theology much, except to disprove through evolutionary theory certain creation myths", you might expand your original answer into fleshing out the debate between creationists and evolutionists, or you might rethink the direction of your answer entirely and talk about the impossibility of locating the physical seat of the soul.

If you have tried both these responses and you are still getting "And...?" it may mean that either the interviewer has a specific response in mind that you simply cannot divine, or they have slipped into a catatonic state. If you have expanded your answers as far as you can take them, or you have looked at the question upside down and back to front, gracefully disengage yourself by asking them to rephrase the problem for you, or simply admit that you do not know what they want and ask them to help you. A simple smile coupled with, 'I'm afraid I don't know, but I'd be really excited to find out,' turns your problem into a virtue, as you seem (and we hope are!) thirsty for new knowledge.

Technical

Sometimes the interviewer is not interested in your personality, your extra curricular activities or whether

or not you had a pleasant trip, they just want to know what you can do with what you know. This is particularly true of Medicine, Maths and Science subjects, but can apply for Social Sciences and Humanities as well. These interviews are supplementary to whatever written tests may already have been done. The best preparation for this kind of interview is a water-tight grasp of the A-Level syllabus, and a willingness to apply that knowledge to new and unknown situations. You should also practise answering questions, drawing diagrams and working out problems on the spot. Candidates who are often most badly caught out by these interviewers are those applying for subjects such as Law, who have been told that 'no previous knowledge of the subject is necessary'. Whilst this is literally true, it is largely intended to mean that Law A-Level is not a necessary precursor to a Law degree. The reasoning behind asking factual questions in such an interview is that any candidate genuinely interested in the subject will have discovered in their own time some of its fundamental principles. A candidate would never be expected to quote specific cases or to know the content of various statutes, but an applicant with no idea of how a Law passes from concept into active use might not look as passionate about their chosen course as their well-informed peers.

Of course, most interviewers will not conform exclusively to any one of the options listed above, but they are likely to demonstrate a mixture of traits associated with each one.

Five Top Qualities

It can be daunting to go into an interview unsure of exactly what qualities are being sought by your interviewer. The following is a list of the top five desirable attributes drawn up in consultation with the ex-admissions tutors on our Advisory Board; these are the real criteria upon which current Oxbridge undergraduates were judged.

1. Subject passion

Perhaps the single most important criterion is passion for your chosen subject. Your interviewer loves their subject enough to have devoted their life's work to it and, if they get the sense of a kindred spirit, your chances of being offered a place will go up immeasurably. Conversely, woe betide the candidate who gives the impression of having chosen their subject by closing their eyes and sticking their finger down on a random page of the prospectus, or because they thought it would be easy to get in.

How do I show it?

Allow your passion to come through in debate, and in the way in which you discuss your subject. Interviewees who speak about aspects of their subject as if they really matter to them come across as having the necessary fervour. Genuinely passionate individuals also tend to be the ones who have picked up a lot of extra-curricular knowledge, as it is easy to learn about something you love. Show the breadth of your extended reading, bring in examples from different books, and actively volunteer new areas for discussion. Finally, try to enjoy the experience! Smile, be enthusiastic and talk openly. If you obviously relish the opportunity to discuss your area of interest with an expert in the field, it will be taken as a good sign of the genuine pleasure you take in your subject. And in fact, if you genuinely do enjoy your subject, you really should relish, notwithstanding a few nerves, the opportunity to discuss your favourite topics with a leading authority on them.

2. Logical, critical and analytical ability

Most Oxbridge graduates are expected at the end of their studies to have developed a rigorous critical mindset. Across the range of subjects, the teaching is designed to instil an enlightened scepticism and an ability to deconstruct presumptions or problems in order to fully understand them. To benefit from this education, an applicant must show the germ of the lateral thinking that makes such analysis possible.

How do I show it?

In verbal exchange the best way to demonstrate these qualities is through a measured and intelligent approach to answering the question (which will often involve breaking it down into its component parts) and a capacity to appreciate different sides of an argument. When a query is put to you, do not answer with the first thing that comes into your head; sit back and try to see why the question has been asked, what the component parts of a response might be, and where the interviewer is leading you. Try and put your ideas in an ordered form before you begin to answer the question.

Whilst these qualities are tested in discussion, many Colleges will issue candidates with a document ten minutes before the interview which will then form the basis for part of the conversation. In an English interview this might be a poem or short story, in History a contemporary letter, a fragment of statute for Law and so on. In each case, the idea will be to test your critical faculties when faced with words or figures on the page. When reading through the document, consider its probable context and wider implications and form as many points and questions as you can in the time given. Pick out concrete detail to reinforce your analysis. It is a candidate's ability to perform close reading, to draw practical conclusions from data, and to see the intended effects of a text - as well as the techniques used to achieve them - that indicates that they possess the necessary analytical qualities.

3. Independent thinking

Knowing everything in the world about your chosen subject will not be enough if that knowledge is not put to original use. Oxbridge seeks to produce independent thinkers who form their own opinions based on analysis of fact.

How do I show it?

Throughout the course of your interview, you should be seeking not only to demonstrate what you know, but also to generate new ideas as your intellect interacts with that of the interviewer. Use the questions as a stimulus to your imagination, and be bold in offering new solutions, suggestions or perspectives. So long as they are based on empirical data, it does not matter whether your comments are ultimately right or wrong. Avoid simply giving extended accounts of other people's theories, or of the plots of books or events of historical periods. It is not enough to demonstrate your skill at memorising and repeating, you must show that you have understood what you have read and formed your own views as a result.

4. Knowledge

Many candidates labour under the misapprehension that the primary purpose of the interview is to test the extent of their knowledge. This is not the case, as knowledge is not a very reliable indicator of academic potential, and a candidate can always learn new facts, whereas the qualities listed above are to some degree intrinsic. Knowledge is still very important however, particularly in Science subjects where the degree course is the natural extension of the A-Level syllabus. It also stands as a good testament to a candidate's commitment. If someone told you they supported Chelsea Football Club, but couldn't name a single player, you might doubt the strength and sincerity of their affection.

How do I show it?

Don't wait to be asked for examples; every point you make should be backed up with a fact. Don't be afraid of taking the interview on a detour. If you are discussing one topic and you suddenly think of an instance in your wider reading that would elucidate your debate or provide a good point of contrast or comparison, bring it in. Interviewers will become quickly irritated if they get the sense that a candidate is rambling or deliberately avoiding direct questions, but will be pleased if you can link disparate pieces of information into a cogent framework. The key to getting this right is relevance- never deploy your knowledge for its own sake, but be sure to use it whenever it is appropriate.

5. Listening and 'teachability'

The admissions interview can be seen as a kind of proto-tutorial, which tests a candidate's suitability for the Oxbridge teaching system. Thus the capacity to listen to and absorb information in this format is essential. As your interviewer may well be responsible for a considerable part of your teaching, there may also be the less abstract consideration of whether they want to work with you specifically.

How do I show it?

Just listen to your interviewer. It is amazing how many candidates do not listen to the question being put to them. If there are any terms or words that you do not understand, do not try to guess, but ask for clarification. Often, if you are working through a complex problem, an interviewer will give you hints and tips to guide you towards a possible solution. Keeping eye contact and attending to the exact words they use can be helpful in formulating your response. If your interviewer makes a particularly forceful or intelligent point, incorporate it into your own argument or use it as a launch pad for further ideas. Ask questions, and try to make the experience as interactive as possible.

Practice Makes...?

Before you go up for the real thing, it's good to get at least one practise interview under your belt, and some candidates will want to do more. Whether you practise your interview technique with teachers, parents, friends, in front of the mirror or with your dog, the basic principle should remain the same - if you feel like you are rehearsing responses, stop. Candidates who are perceived as 'trained' by interviewers, or who deliver over-rehearsed answers, tend to fare badly because they often seem intellectually inflexible. They have set notions of which questions to expect, and are thus tempted to foist pre-prepared answers and topics of discussion onto the interviewer, regardless of whether or not they are entirely appropriate. In all our research into past questions, it is the differences between them that have been most apparent. The common factor lies in the kind of critical thinking required to produce a decent response. A practice interview can help you bring your intelligence to bear more easily on complex or unfamiliar problems without allowing nerves or confusion to get in the way, and will help you spot any tics or areas of weakness in advance.

Je Ne Regrette Rien

Here, as an afterthought, are some of the most commonly cited regrets voiced by our clients after the dust has settled. Make sure they don't become yours!

"I wouldn't have been so nervous- I would have been more forceful in discussion."

It is easy in retrospect to curse the timidity of your former self, and an interview is always less frightening in memory than in the imagination. However, many of the candidates who were least happy with their experience felt that the chance to shine had passed them by due to a simple excess of nerves. Screaming 'RELAX!' at yourself as you wait outside the study may not have the desired effect and, if breathing techniques simply cause you to hyperventilate, you may just have to reconcile yourself to the fact that you will go in to the interview a little frightened. This is not in itself a problem, so long as you remember to do three things. Firstly, defend your opinions and state your views, using concrete evidence wherever possible. Do not be scared away from an argument by the stress and formality of the occasion. Secondly, don't let nerves cloud your passion for your subject. If you are visibly suffering for the duration of the conversation, your interviewer might not get a sufficient impression of enthusiasm! Finally, if you are confronted with a tough question, never be afraid to ask for a minute to think. This lets your interviewer know that you are properly considering your responses rather than just opening your mouth and seeing which phrases wander out first. It can also give you a much-needed breather in which to collect your thoughts and restore your equanimity.

"I wish I'd reread the books I mentioned in my personal statement."

You will, of course, immediately look under-prepared and unenthusiastic if you are ignorant of something you mentioned on your personal statement. The long wait between the composition of your personal statement and your interview means that books and ideas that were fresh at the time of writing can become a little stale. It is worth checking all the details of the novels, texts and theories you've mentioned, as you have effectively invited your interviewer to ask you questions on those topics. Maintaining a folder with a side of A4 on each book you have read is a good idea and at the very least going through these provides a useful way to occupy the half-hour countdown to your interview.

"I wish I'd read the newspapers more regularly."

The extent to which current affairs are relevant to your interview will depend on the subject for which you are applying. Anyone wanting to read Politics, History, Law or Medicine should read the newspapers extensively in the weeks approaching their interview (and, ideally, before that). Modern languages students should make sure they have a good working knowledge of recent events in the countries where their chosen languages are spoken.

"I wish I'd learnt more Maths!"

Of all the subjects for which we helped candidates to apply, the one which was most technically tested at interview was Maths. Many applicants expected a discussion about their subject, and were greeted instead with half an hour of complex problem solving, sometimes on a white board in front of the interviewing panel. Budding Mathematicians should ensure they are well versed in unseen problem solving, and are prepared if their interview shies away from the theoretical and concentrates solely on the practical. They should also get used to discussing problems verbally and explaining their reasoning as well as working them through on the page (or board).

5

Interview questions

Nobody Expects the Spanish Inquisition

With each new year of interviews, a selection of articles appears in the national (and international) press covering the obscure, bizarre and downright surreal inquiries fired off by academics at bemused 17 year-olds. No one, from future Physicists to hopeful Historians, is safe from the potential dangers of the weird and wonderful question. This chapter includes a few of those, together with a few more normal queries, with a view to showing you what kinds of things our previous clients have encountered. The point of this exercise is not to tell you what questions you will be asked, or indeed to suggest that there is any standardised approach to generating such questions. Rather, the sample answers are designed to show you how, with the right mentality, you can engage in a critical approach to any question, and keep your head when dealing with the tougher intellectual challenges an interview may generate. Factual questions and questions directly related to your personal statement and areas of interest will of course feature in the real interviews, and you should not read anything into their absence from the following list. It is impractical in the case of the former, and impossible in the case of the latter, to give any space to such questions here. Whilst only ten popular subjects from Oxbridge are covered below, you will benefit from reading each one whether or not it pertains to your course, as there are certain common principles that transcend even the Sciences/Humanities divide.

The Dangers of the Wild Stab

'Cultural imperialism', 'counter-factual historicism', 'Arnoldian touchstones'; if you know the meanings of all these technical terms and phrases, you know more than 99% of your fellow students. In any given interview, there is a fairly good chance that a word or expression you haven't come across before will be used. Remember that though you may not understand the word, you will almost certainly be able to understand the concept. Always ask your interviewer to clarify or explain unknown terms. It won't reflect badly on you, and it may save you from making what will appear to be a really silly answer.

"How would you judge a work to be canonical?" English, Cambridge

One of the central problems to Music, Art History and Literature is the establishment of objective criteria of worth. How can we say that this poem is better than that one, and argue our case in such a way as to have universal and clear points of judgement? This question is designed to guide the student towards deciding what it is that gives a piece of literature durability and makes it worthy of ongoing critical attention and, by extension, what makes a great work. As with so many of these questions there is no right answer, but you might construct the beginnings of a response around several different points. Firstly, what do we understand by 'canon'? One definition is the list of texts, authorised by critical consensus (as far as such a thing is ever possible), which form the core of English literature for study at Secondary School and beyond. Good ways to judge whether or not a work should be considered canonical might therefore include asking: Does the work spread a pattern of influence which makes an understanding of it necessary to the literature that follows? Does it embody the spirit of an age, in form, in content or in language? We might say of Chaucer's 'Canterbury Tales', for example, that it is considered canonical as a result of the scope of genre from courtly epic to fabliau, the coverage of all strata of contemporary English society, and the vision of a language reconciling a Latinate and Germanic vocabulary, a bridge between modern and old English. Does the book continue to be widely read and studied? Is the author part of some particular movement, of which this is one of the defining works? Does reading and understanding the text impart a strong moral, aesthetic or political truth? Does the text support numerous different interpretations? These are just some of the kinds of questions you might ask of such a work to judge whether or not it is canonical. As there is no complete answer, but rather a series of possible considerations, this query provides an excellent opportunity to form a rapport with your interviewer. If you begin by making one intelligent point, they may well ask you further questions to help you refine your definition, leading you into a lengthy and enjoyable discussion.

"Is defending women's rights in Afghanistan a form of cultural imperialism?" Archaeology and Anthropology, Cambridge

The candidate is being asked to examine the assumptions upon which their own socio-political views may be based, and to attempt to engage objectively with other cultural values. The interviewee must be able to take a step back from what they believe, however passionately, and consider the answer rationally. What is interesting about this question is the conflict it creates between two traditional liberal principles, the rights of women and the rights of individual societies to determine their own nature. A good argument to disprove the statement implicit in the question might begin by establishing, as far as is possible, the idea that the defence of women's rights is not a western cultural construct but an absolute moral imperative that transcends national identity, and that attempting to do so is therefore justified regardless of the domestic circumstances. A counter argument might revolve around the idea that you cannot by definition impose liberation of any kind on a society- some cultural theorists have written extensively on the differences between colonial nations that achieve independence through internal revolt and through external withdrawal, arguing that only the former can pave the way for psychological healing from the experience of being treated as second class. The internal contradictions of 'Operation Free Iraq' might provide a good source of concrete detail for such a theoretical debate. A candidate could go on to suggest that it would be more appropriate, in the light of this analysis, to try and stimulate a national awareness of women's rights through education or providing funding for locally run projects.

"In a society of angels do you need Law?" Jurisprudence, Oxford

Angels would be incapable of committing sin, but they might commit parking violations- if all the streets of heaven were blocked with double-parked Porsches, none of the heavenly host would be able to get anywhere and the society would eventually grind to halt. This question will lead a good candidate towards a distinction between what is legal and what is moral. The point can be made from either direction- a variant on the theme is asking why adultery isn't illegal, but is considered immoral. Negotiating this type of question requires the makings of a legal brain, and of a good student of Jurisprudence, the theory of Law, which is the official title of the Oxford course. Show that you understand the difference between right and legal, between the laws that facilitate the orderly transactions of a healthy society and the laws which prohibit moral transgressions, and you will prove you have the ability to grasp the fundamental theoretical discussions on which the Law course is based.

"Would the life of a man stuck in a box being fed experiences that he believed were real by a computer be as complete as a man living in the real world?"
PPE, Oxford

This is a tricky question, and one that cannot be answered if you are preoccupied with being 'right' (if you can correctly divine the exact nature of reality in a half hour interview, you really don't need to worry about University anyway). The temptation with these hypothetical queries (sometimes called 'thought experiments') is to pick at the scenario: 'how could he be born in the box?', 'what computer could do this?', etc., and this must be resisted. Instead, look at some of the key terms such as 'experiences' or 'real world', and begin to work up ideas around them. It can be helpful to generate answers in the form of further questions. Do we have to assume a man's 'experiences' are the sum total of his 'life', or are there more complex issues, such as 'purpose' or 'achievement'? Since we know the world exclusively through the medium of our senses, can we really claim our world is any more 'real' than the box-man's? Is life given meaning by the reactions of those around us, and if so can we call the existence of someone perpetually alone 'complete'? By breaking the question down into manageable chunks, you can begin to tackle it logically.

Another possible answer is to give some accounts of different philosophical perspectives. A solipsist might say yes, as the self is all that is or ever can be truly known. An existentialist might say yes, if the man constructed his box-life upon a self-generated code of behaviour and rigidly adhered to its principles and so on. This answer could then be augmented, as always with Philosophy (and, in fact, all subjects) by adding your own view. One approach demonstrates a strong capacity for independent thought, the other a good working knowledge of the spectrum of philosophical thought.

"How would you spend £6 million improving the NHS?"
Medicine, Oxford

A question like this provides a good opportunity to demonstrate that you would not only make a good scientist, but a good doctor. You may dazzle an interviewer with your grasp of chemistry and anatomy, but if you do not demonstrate a solid interest in the way Medicine is practised you may miss out on an offer simply because your interviewer doubts your commitment to becoming a practitioner. The academic standard of Medical applications is extremely high so a good answer might set you apart from the crowd.

Perhaps the first answer to this question is 'It wouldn't go very far!' £6M is a relatively small amount in budgetary terms for a national service. Focus, therefore, on one particular point or issue you have encountered in the media or in the course of your studies or work experience, and make your improvement in that specific area. If, for example, you have heard about a new screening technique for breast cancer that allows earlier detection, you may say you would like to invest in that. If the recent revelation of an increase in cases of M.R.S.A. in hospitals caught your attention, you might say you wished to spend the money implementing better hygiene procedures.

The question appears daunting because of its open-endedness, but you should see a query like this as a golden opportunity to demonstrate an awareness of any current medical issue, from nurses' pay to groundbreaking gene therapies. A good answer also requires a clear structure. State your choice, explain it, and then go on to say why it should be prioritised over the many other pressing financial needs of the National Health Service.

"Would you give a liver transplant to an otherwise healthy 75 year old woman?" Medicine, Cambridge

Many medical applicants are surprised to be confronted for the first time in their interviews by questions of medical ethics. Such questions can take many forms, but are often phrased around realistic hypothetical situations- should we prosecute those who help terminally ill loved ones to die? Should we deny treatment to someone who has exacerbated a condition through deliberate lifestyle choices, such as smoking or allowing themselves to become morbidly obese? How would you counsel a patient resisting treatment on religious grounds? These ethical debates are often a good opportunity to bring in concrete details from recent stories you have been following in the papers. The placement of a 'do not resuscitate' order on baby Charlotte Wyatt, for example, brought to the fore arguments over whether it should be the courts, the family or doctors who have the ultimate say over a patient's fate. Again, there is no easy answer to these questions, but you can divide your response into the scientific and the ethical. What are the post-operative survival rates for liver recipients? How dramatically are these affected by the age of the patient? Are there other treatment options available? Under the ethical section, you might like to consider such issues as whether it is ever justifiable to discriminate on the grounds of age, and whether we can distinguish between age and a patient's general suitability for transplant. Alternatively, given the limited availability of donor organs, is it justifiable to apportion treatment to someone younger or with more dependants? Is it a physician's place to make these kinds of judgements? There may also be a legal angle to consider (GMC guidelines recommend a cut-off point of 65 for liver transplants). A good trick for avoiding trouble when responding to these issues is to outline two possible sides of a debate before stating your personal opinion. This will prevent you from weighing in on one side, only to find yourself fighting a rearguard action against your interviewer on behalf of the other.

"How many 0's are at the end of 30! (30 factorial)?"
Maths, Oxford

The first thing to realise here is that the number in question is huge and that the method is NOT going to be to calculate it. So we must look for a shortcut. The idea is to think of the factors which go together to produce a zero, namely '2' and '5'. We then look at how many of each we have. All the even numbers up to 30 will contribute at least one 2 so we have a great many of these. Similarly, all the multiples of 5 will contribute at least one 5. These are: 5, 10, 15, 20, 25 and 30. 25, however, contributes two 5s so we have 5^7 and 2^x in the prime factorisation where x is greater than 15 (number of even numbers less than or equal to 30). 7, then, is clearly the limiting factor and we can conclude that there are seven 0s in 30! Try generalising this for n! (n factorial). (Note that this would probably be a bit much to ask at interview).

"What provides the lift to keep aeroplanes aloft? How do aeroplanes fly upside-down?" Physics, Oxford

The popular/traditional answer to part a) involves the application of Bernoulli's Principle to the airflow over the curved cross-section of the aircraft wing, arguing that this creates a region above the curved upper surface of the wing which is at a lower pressure than the region under the wing, thus creating lift from the difference in pressure.

Whilst there is some element of truth in the application of Bernoulli's Principle to the problem of aircraft lift, it is a fact that aeroplanes can and do fly inverted at aerobatic displays, and this inverted flight cannot be explained using the above.

The explanation lies instead with Newton's Third Law: For every action there is an equal and opposite reaction. Consider the "angle-of-attack", i.e. the angle made between the wing and the oncoming air-flow. If the front edge of the wing is raised slightly compared to the trailing edge, the oncoming air will be deflected downwards off the underside of the wing, causing the wing (and hence plane) to be lifted in the opposite direction to the deflected air. This is how planes can fly inverted if the pilot correctly adjusts the angle of the plane and its wings.

There are therefore a number of factors involved in the explanation of how planes generate lift. To explore this topic in more detail, you might like to start by browsing the Aeronautics Learning Laboratory website at www.allstar.fiu.edu.

General Principles

If you have read all or several of the above sample responses, you may notice the emergence of certain common factors. Firstly, there is seldom a right answer. Even where there is a correct response, as in certain science questions, it requires the imaginative application of relatively basic knowledge - it is the thinking behind the question, not the obscurity of the data needed, that is the challenge and what is being looked for. Because there is no correct response, a successful candidate should try to free up their thinking to generate a number of reasonable options. Often, a good way to initiate this is by voicing the further questions that the original question poses. When entering into an issue which looks likely to generate a debate, don't shy away from giving an opinion, but cover yourself by offering both sides of the argument before definitely settling for one. Admit that you will probably encounter ideas you had never before considered- you cannot prepare for the interviews by covering every possible subject of discussion. Rather you should relax, and treat the questions you get with the same calm, rational and critical eye you would turn to any new problem.

Finally, the above responses include several concrete examples. These are not intended to represent things a good candidate or indeed any candidate should know before they go into interview. They are simply designed to make the general point that, wherever possible, theoretical debate must be grounded in concrete fact. You don't have to have the encyclopaedia memorised to give some examples, and lend your arguments the stamp of authority. If you deploy your knowledge of current affairs, history and extra-curricular reading effectively, you can make a little go a long way, regardless of your intended discipline.

Questions, Questions

Here are a few of the past questions gleaned over years of research from actual Oxford and Cambridge interviews. You may never encounter anything like these again, but someone who is now an Oxbridge undergraduate did, and gave a good enough answer to secure a place. Have a go at answering the ones for your subject, paying special attention to ideas of structure and analytical thought.

N.B. There are a number of types of questions that have been largely ignored for the purposes of this section, either because they require the printing of additional documents, diagrams or formulae, or because they relate to subjects of interest mentioned on individual UCAS forms. Thus every candidate should expect, in addition to the more general types of questions listed here, to encounter a text or other source on which to pass comment, a problem to solve or a sheet of data to analyse.

They should also expect extensive questioning based on the areas of interest listed in the Personal Statement.

Archaeology and Anthropology

- Where do you think the Elgin Marbles should be, London or Athens?
- Why do we still celebrate Christmas? What do you think makes Christmas such a long-lasting and widely celebrated holiday? Why is it so special?
- How does studying History link with Archaeology?

Architecture

- How much do you think architecture changes views in society?
- Who would you say is the most important architectural writer?
- What is the importance of light in architecture?

Anglo-Saxon, Norse and Celtic

- What is the difference between literature and history?

- How can we date a source if we don't know when or by whom it was written?
- Which ASNaC papers are you looking forward to studying most?

Biochemistry

- What are the differences between a human enzyme and the enzymes of bacteria that live in a hot spring?
- How does DNA fingerprinting work? What is its use?
- How do amino acids behave in both acidic and basic conditions?

Biological Sciences

- What is a mitochondrion? Why do you only inherit mitochondrial genes from your mother?
- Why is carbon of such importance in living systems?
- Why are big, fierce animals so rare?

Chemistry

- What makes drugs physiologically active?
- Write down an organic reaction you have studied at school and explain its mechanism.
- How would you calculate the inter-atomic spacing of particles in this room?

Classics

- Do you think that Tacitus was biased in his writings and, if so, does that render them useless?
- Are history and myth compatible?
- What underlying messages are there in the Aeneid suggesting that Rome and its foundations were not very secure?

Earth Sciences

- What do you believe would be the major differences on Earth if:
    a) no atmosphere had ever formed?
    b) there was no water?
    c) plate tectonics did not exist?
- What would you expect to see at a compressional/extensional/passive margin?
- List a number of different possible methods for dating a rock specimen.

Economics and Management

- Consider a production line. What could be done to help the worker to get away from the routine?
- Discuss the interaction between fiscal and monetary policy.
- Why do Rolls-Royce build cars by hand, and Toyota by machine?

Economics

- Should governments subsidise agriculture?
- Relate Keynes' work to the dot-com boom.
- What's the difference between a correlation and a cause and effect relationship?

Egyptology

- What first interested you in Egyptology?
- How was Egyptian mythology recorded?
- Describe how the Egyptians preserved their dead.

Engineering

- Show the forces acting on a ladder.

- If you had a cylinder, sealed at both ends, with the pressure rising inside, would it blow at the end or split along the side first?
- At what altitude h above the North Pole is the weight of an object reduced to one half of its value on a the Earth's surface? Assume the Earth to be a sphere radius R and express h as a fraction of R.

English

- Read and try to date this short, anonymous poem. Who do you think might have written it? Comment on the imagery used and its effect; does this poem remind you of anything you've read?
- What is the difference between a simile and a comparison?
- What is tragedy?

Experimental Psychology

- How is it that a painting by a four year old of "a tiger amongst tulips" (as described by the child) doesn't look like a tiger despite the child studying a tiger at the zoo the day before and being satisfied with the outcome?
- If a man has no hair (n) he is called bald. If we add hairs to his head using the formula n+1, he would still be called bald. Is this correct?
- Discuss the origin of phobias (nature vs. nurture).

Geography

- What are the advantages for retailers to concentrate their activities in malls rather than disperse through towns?
- Do you have an interest in saving the environment? What evidence is there for human influences on climate?

- If you could take a non-geographer anywhere in the world to convince them geography was important, where would you go and what would you say?

History and Politics

- Is national character a useful concept in history?
- How can one define a revolution?
- How would you differentiate between power and authority?

History of Art

- What is your opinion on the Turner Prize and Brit Art?
- Discuss restoration and conservation. Are they a worthwhile investment?
- What work of art would you most like to own?

History

- Would history be worth studying if it didn't repeat itself?
- How do today's interpretations of democratic values differ from those of 19th century and how have they evolved?
- How does a historian gather information?

Human Sciences

- Design an experiment to show whether monkeys' behaviour is innate or learnt.
- Can/do animals have language?
- What is the future of GM crops?

Japanese

- 'I ran into a woman carrying flowers' - where are the ambiguities in that sentence? Have you noticed any instances in Japanese where ambiguities such as these occur?

- What major differences do you see between Japanese and British cultures? Can you think of anything that makes the two cultures seem similar?
- What first interested you in the study of the Japanese language?

Land Economy

- Why are wages higher in London?
- What do you think are the implications for shopping with the phenomenon of the internet?
- If someone is acquitted in Criminal proceedings, can they, and should they, still be liable to be sued in Civil Law?

Law / Jurisprudence

- If A gave B £100 thinking it was a loan and B accepted the money thinking it was a gift, should he have to give it back?
- Smith sees Jones walking towards the edge of a cliff. Smith knows Jones is blind, but doesn't like him, so allows him to walk off the edge. Is this murder?
- Should judges have a legislative role?

Maths

- Prove that $n^2 - 1$ is divisible by 8 for all odd integers n.
- A body with mass m is falling towards earth with speed v. It has a drag force equal to kv. Set up a differential equation and solve it for v.
- Prove that any number consists of prime factors or is a prime number.

Medicine

- What interests you most about current advances in medical technology?

- Why is it that cancer cells are more susceptible to destruction by radiation than normal cells?
- What is the normal level of potassium? What is it used for? How does it move in and out of cells?

Modern Languages

- Why do you want to study a very literature-based degree?
- Do you notice any differences between English and European literature? If so, why might these exist?
- Discuss current affairs issues relevant to the countries you hope to study.

Natural Sciences

- Discuss ways in which plants adapt to dry conditions.
- When an ice cube melts in a glass of water, does the water level increase, decrease or stay the same?
- Which reaches the bottom of a slope faster, a ball rolling down the slope, or a ball sliding down the slope?

Oriental Studies

- Give me a brief case study of an area of Middle Eastern politics that has interested you.
- How many cultures are grouped together under the label "China"?
- Please construct a sentence using the word 'up' as a verb.

Physics

- Explain how we know a centripetal force exists and how we can prove the presence of this force.
- Why is it not strictly true to say that one planet orbits another?

- Why does metal expand when it's heated?

Physiology
- What do you understand by the term "all or nothing"?
- What ways can you think of for a molecule to cross a cell membrane?
- What is the main function of the nervous system?

Politics, Philosophy and Economics
- Can faith in quantum physics and invisible forces tie in with faith in an invisible God?
- Why do you think communism was unsuccessful in the Russian countryside?
- What are the origins of wage inflation?

Social and Political Sciences
- Is there tension between British Nationalism and local patriotism?
- Does the welfare state trap people into poverty?
- Should children always be educated in a co-ed environment?

Theology
- Do the Gods command it because it is great, or is it great because the Gods command it?
- What are the moral implications, if any, of voluntary euthanasia?
- What is the best reason you can think of for believing in God? Do you think this course could be persuasive on the matter?

Veterinary Science
- Is selective breeding tantamount to genetic modification?

- Can you describe an experiment to differentiate between a normal and a multi-resistant strain of bacteria?
- Discuss the mechanisms underlying sensory adaptation.

And Finally...

If the above questions are not enough for you, and you feel the need to pit your wits against something a little more obscure, here are a few other gems our candidates encountered in their interviews since 2000...

- "Are Prime Ministers becoming more presidential in style?" Modern History and Politics, Ox
- "Compare these bottles of Tesco and Timotei Shampoo." Law, Ox
- "Convince me to watch you do a dance performance." Philosophy, Cam
- "Define irony." Classics, Ox
- "Devise an equation to estimate the number of aeroplanes in the sky." Natural Sciences, Cam
- "Do you know what economics was called before it was called economics?" Economics, Cam
- "Do you think the Bavarian peasants of 1848 had an ideology?" History, Cam
- "Does a computer have a conscience?" Law, Cam
- "Don't you agree that Shakespeare was a waste of time and totally irrelevant to today?" Modern and Medieval Languages, Cam
- "How does Berlin compare to Dusseldorf?" History of Art, Cam
- "How many atoms are there in a brussel sprout?" Natural Sciences, Cam
- "How many molecules are there in this room?" Natural Sciences, Cam

- "How would you define a book?" Philosophy, Politics and Economics, Ox
- "How would you measure the weight of your own head?" Medicine, Cam
- "If there was an omnipotent god would he be able to create a stone that he couldn't lift?" Classics, Ox
- "Is 'Taggart' an accurate portrayal of Glasgow?" English, Ox
- "Is altruism dead?" Social and Political Sciences, Cam
- "Is the chair really there?" Philosophy, Cam
- "Is the moon made of cheese?" Veterinary Sciences, Cam
- "Shipwrecked sailors are forced to eat a shipmate. Is this a crime?" Law, Cam
- "What are cricket bats made of?" Medicine, Cam
- "What factors have affected Irish emigration to Norwich?" Social and Political Sciences, Cam
- "What has been the most significant event of your life so far?" Geography, Cam
- "What is your favourite line from Henry V?" English, Ox
- "What questions would you like us to ask you?" Medicine, Cam
- "Why are we here?" Medicine, Ox
- "Why do seals exhale before they dive under water?" Natural Sciences, Cam
- "Why is this piece of string red?" Natural Sciences, Cam

Visit our website at **www.oxbridgeapplications.com** for a much longer list of questions.

Oxbridge and the politics of entrance

The Popular Conception of Oxbridge

"I loathe these people. They've all been to Oxbridge University, wherever the hell that is, and they walk around in their open-toed sandals going, 'You can't say that, you can't do this, do you like my glasses, they're like John Lennon's?" - Alan Partridge

If you are applying to Oxford or Cambridge University, the only criterion on which you will be selected is your own academic merit. However, in the current climate the Oxbridge brand name can occasionally work against the Universities it represents. In a society where inclusiveness, transparency and equality are increasingly the cardinal virtues, the air of mystery and privilege which envelopes Oxbridge is beginning to attract strong criticism, and risks alienating certain sections of society.

This is borne out by the admission statistics. Less than 10% of British children are privately educated and yet they make they make up almost 50% of the Oxbridge student body. However, the acceptance rate for state and independent schools is actually very similar (30% and 24% respectively). The cause, therefore, of state school students being under-represented at Oxbridge must be with the number of applications in the first place. This confusion between admission and acceptance rates has brought Oxbridge a great deal of undeserved criticism.

Oxford 2006 Admisssions

	Applications			Acceptances			Success Rate (%)		
	Male	**Female**	**All**	**Male**	**Female**	**All**	**Male**	**Female**	**All**
Maintained	3,017	2,983	6,000	792	739	1,531	26.3	24.8	25.5
Independent	2,261	2,039	4,300	762	629	1,391	33.7	30.8	32.3
Other*	1,133	1,181	2,314	155	151	306	13.7	12.8	13.2
TOTAL	**6,411**	**6,203**	**12,614**	**1,709**	**1,519**	**3,228**	**26.7**	**24.5**	**25.6**

Cambridge 2006 Admisssions

	Applications			Acceptances			Success Rate (%)		
	Male	**Female**	**All**	**Male**	**Female**	**All**	**Male**	**Female**	**All**
Maintained	3,228	3,325	6,553	759	795	1,554	23.5	23.9	23.7
Independent	2,055	1,998	4,053	665	675	1,340	32.4	33.8	33.1
Other*	1,681	1,807	3,488	208	237	445	12.4	13.1	12.8
TOTAL	**6,964**	**7,130**	**14,094**	**1,632**	**1,707**	**3,339**	**23.4**	**23.9**	**23.7**

* Mainly International

    The truth is that both Oxford and Cambridge are working hard to change public perception of the Oxbridge brand, but with seven hundred years of history behind them, it is inevitably a slow process. Unfortunately, one of its main effects thus far has been to frighten the middle classes and those who have sent their children to private schools, who are resistant to the idea of the proactive widening of access because they feel cheated of the effort and money they have poured into their own children's education with a view to giving them the best possible chance of entrance to a top university. Thus admissions tutors at the two universities find themselves caught in a pincer movement by the Oxbridge brand, between accusations of elitism on the one hand, and of positive discrimination on the other.

Both Universities are taking active measures to combat the widespread perception of elitism and it is essential that the larger public take notice of these efforts, and embrace them. You, however, should try to forget the brand (and forgive the name of our organisation and book!) You will be applying to Oxford or Cambridge University, and the only criterion on which you will be selected is your personal merit. To maximise your chances before the interview, every candidate should accept this basic principle, and begin to consider how best to display that slippery term, 'merit'.

The common misconception of the Oxbridge brand works both ways- many students feel discouraged from applying not only because they fear the University would dislike them, but because they themselves would dislike the university. The truth is that, unless you positively resist attempts to draw you into college and university life, you will eventually find friends like yourself or, even more excitingly, friends who are completely different. To give an extreme example of the degree to which the Universities try to foster a thriving social life amongst its students, Cambridge RAG annually beats its own record for the largest collective blind date in the world!

The public perception of Oxbridge is slowly changing, and coming into line with what has long been the truth- that the universities are, as far as possible, pure meritocracies. To draw a useful analogy, imagine that Manchester United football team began to select its players for some quality other than their ability to play football. What would happen to their position in the Premiership over the following seasons? Oxbridge have consistently achieved the most impressive undergraduate and post-graduate results in the country. They do not keep this position by allowing sub-standard applicants to matriculate.

The Circus of Entrance

In 2000 Laura Spence, a pupil from a northern grammar school with five As at A-Level, was refused a place to read Medicine at Magdalen College, Oxford. The subsequent row, which raged from pub to high table to Prime Minister's Question Time, brought many hidden grievances to the fore. At Oxford itself, the student population reacted strongly against her school's decision to take the story to the media.

The incident marked a distinct shift in Oxbridge's fortunes, as it underlined the increasing politicisation of the admissions process, and gave the scent of blood to newspaper editors. Much of the prurient journalistic attention that Oxbridge has received since, from stories of pole-dancing girls at Queens', Cambridge, to excessive drinking and on-stage sex acts at Oxford, can be traced back to the spirit of the media furore over Laura Spence. Much of the more serious debate about access, from the austere presence of the regulatory body Ofsted (wittily nick-named 'Off-toff') to the president of Trinity College Michael Beloff's recent threat of privatisation and his call to the government to 'get its tanks off our lawns' also owes something to that fateful rejection letter.

At the time of the Laura Spence case the Chancellor Gordon Brown called the incident an 'absolute disgrace', citing the fact that she had been accepted by Harvard on the strength of her five As as proof of Oxford's class prejudice in refusing her a place. As so often where stories about Oxbridge are concerned, the media coverage and spin that was given to the incident completely missed the point. The fact that all the applicants who did receive offers were similarly qualified (and, in many cases, from similar backgrounds); the fact that she was rejected by Oxford for Medicine and accepted by Harvard for Biochemistry (Medicine being a highly vocational subject, where real commitment to becoming a doctor is tested at interview); and finally the fact that hundreds of talented candidates from all strata of society are rejected by Oxbridge every year (if they didn't have good academic grades, why bother applying?). The absurdity of it all was underlined when, in an interview with the Daily Mail, Spence herself said, "I never doubted Oxford's decision. I was a bit upset when I came out of the interview because I knew I hadn't done as well as I thought I could have." The government high-jacked the issue in order to pursue its own agenda of higher education reform.

The spectre of rigged admissions was again raised when a journalist for the Sunday Times convinced a tutor at Pembroke College, Oxford to take their child on the understanding that the college would receive a £300,000 donation. Rev. Dr John Platt admitted the possibility of the deal with the hubristic words 'if you're going to keep it absolutely, totally confidential, the answer is: in the past it has been done, okay?' The members of staff involved were both immediately suspended, amply demonstrating the seriousness with which such incidents are viewed. Even with the donation, Rev. Dr Platt still indicated that the reporter's child would need at least two As and a B at A-level.

Unfortunately, it is examples such as the ones given above that tend to shape public perception of the Oxbridge admissions process. The stories of corruption and prejudice, real and imagined, are simply more interesting than the thousands of well-conducted interviews that have taken place over the past centuries. Clearing your head of such images is one of the best preparations for the Oxbridge interview. In fact, on proper consideration, the existence of rare stories like those above serves to illustrate two things: the public's fascination with Oxford and Cambridge and the exceptionally high regard in which places at those two universities are held.

The Real Story

It will never be possible to entirely eliminate the element of subjectivity from the interview process, nor would that be desirable. For teacher and student to get the most from the tutorial system, they have to be able to form a rapport. By pooling candidates, Oxford and Cambridge ensure that they maintain the flexibility to accommodate individuals who may not get on with interviewers in their chosen college, but still possess the necessary intelligence and commitment to benefit from an Oxbridge education. Sometimes, in isolated incidents, applicants have had bad experiences. Interviewers are only human, and academics can have bad days like the rest of us.

Finally

If you've made it this far and taken on board some, or all, of the above advice, you will already be well on your way and the final part will be up to you. However, here are a few additional tools which you can use either to fine tune your application or simply to make the whole process that little bit more interesting

About the Company

Oxbridge Applications is an education consultancy which helps bright students achieve their potential when applying to the universities of Oxford and Cambridge. Founded in 1999, by Oxbridge graduates to demystify the Oxbridge selection process, we have helped over 30,000 students with their applications and have a success rate of 45% compared with the average Oxbridge success rate of just 26%. Every year we work with more than 200 schools from both the state (68%) and independent (32%) sectors.

Much of our work with state schools is funded by government schemes, such as Aimhigher, in order to promote excellence and widen participation in higher education. We now work with ~10% of all Oxbridge applicants every year. We run nationwide events to educate, inspire and equip students. We do not believe that candidates can in any way be coached, trained or rehearsed for success, but we do believe that they should be aware of what admissions tutors are really looking for. Our Access Scheme ensures that all applicants can benefit from our expertise, regardless of income. We split our support into three main areas:

1. Oxbridge Advantage: Free Information Online

To learn more about the Oxbridge admissions process we would recommend that, in addition to this book, prospective applicants, parents and teachers consult the University prospectuses and attend University Faculty, College and General Open Days.

Further to these valuable resources, please take a look at our website (**www.oxbridgeapplications.com**), which is being updated in 2007. On this site applicants can find additional details and insider knowledge on the Oxbridge application process. They can also visit the exclusive Oxbridge Applications Members' Area - a free online tool which provides access to our library of free online resources including:

- Choosing between Oxford and Cambridge
- Guidance on selecting a college
- Advice on personal statements
- Recent interview questions
- A free interview preparation guide

2. Interview and Admissions Test Preparation Events

If you would like to benefit from extra help with your interview preparation or with admissions tests (LNAT, BMAT, UKCAT, HAT), Oxbridge Applications runs a series of events during which offers applicants the opportunity to hear talks from ex-Oxbridge admissions tutors as well as receive subject-specific interviews with Oxbridge graduates.

The Interview Preparation Weekend is held on the final weekend of October and a series of Interview Preparation Days and Admissions Test Preparation Days take place in London, Birmingham, Bristol and Manchester throughout October, November and into December. Students in receipt of the EMA may be eligible to join our Access Scheme. For more information regarding our Access Scheme and these events please either visit **www.oxbridgeapplications.com** or call us on **020 7499 2394**.